CARB CYCLING

Cookbook

Your Key to Fitness: A Complete Guide to Low & High Carb Meals, Effective Exercise Plans, and Easy Ways to Lose Weight, Build Muscle, and Get in Shape with Two 30-Day Meal Plans

Mark L. Shaw

✸ HERE IS YOU FREE GIFT!
🖐 SCAN HERE TO DOWNLOAD IT

1. All fitness levels welcome. Start at your level, push your boundaries.
2. Detailed guidance ensures injury-free, effective workouts.
3. Gym, home, full-body, the complete wellness package. Enhance your diet, boost wellness.

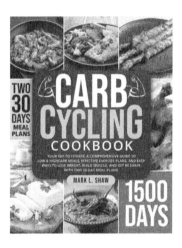

🖐 SCAN HERE TO DOWNLOAD IT FOR FREE

Table of content

Chapter 7

Introduction

Welcome to the journey of exploring Carb Cycling, A dietary approach that has seen increasing attention and intrigue in recent years. As we continue to broaden our understanding of nutrition and its profound impact on our health and well-being, new paradigms are constantly being introduced, shedding light on innovative ways to achieve our fitness and wellness goals. One such approach is carb cycling, a concept that dances on the cutting-edge of dietary science, merging the benefits of both high-carb and low-carb regimens to offer a flexible and potent tool for optimizing health, boosting athletic performance, and enhancing body composition.

The essence of carb cycling lies in the art of variation – adjusting our intake of carbohydrates in line with our body's needs and activity levels. By doing so, it seeks to harness the best of both worlds: the energy-sustaining, muscle-building power of carbohydrates and the fat-burning potential of a low-carb, ketogenic state. But like all tools, carb cycling needs to be understood and applied correctly to reap its full benefits. This is where our journey in this book begins.

Carb Cycling is designed to be your comprehensive guide on this nutritional journey. It does not merely present you with a dietary template to follow, but rather, it aims to equip you with a deep understanding of your body's metabolic processes, allowing you to tailor your diet to your unique needs and goals.

This book has been meticulously structured to progressively build your knowledge. Beginning with the basics, we delve into the nitty-gritty of carb cycling, shedding light on what it is, its potential benefits, and the important considerations to bear in mind before embarking on this dietary journey. We then move on to the practical aspects, assisting you in assessing your goals, determining your carb intake for various days, and calculating your overall macronutrient requirements.

Further, the book will guide you through the strategies for high-carb days, emphasizing their significance in fueling performance and the role of low-carb days in promoting fat loss. To take things a notch higher, we explore the concept of no-carb and very low-carb days, aimed at enhancing ketosis and insulin sensitivity, along with practical strategies for transitioning into and out of these phases.

The journey continues as we dive into a world of recipes, each crafted to nourish and tantalize your taste buds while keeping you true to your carb cycling regime. They cover the entire spectrum of your daily meals, including breakfast, lunch, dinner, and even snacks and desserts, with options for both high-carb and low-carb days.

In the concluding chapter, you will find two meticulously designed 30-day meal plans – one high-carb and one low-carb – that you can either follow as is or use as a blueprint to design your own. To make the process easier and more efficient, we provide a list of useful apps for calorie calculation and a complete shopping list encompassing all the ingredients used in the recipes.

This book is more than just a guide. It is a companion in your quest to understand and harness the power of carb cycling. Whether you are an athlete aiming for peak performance, a fitness enthusiast seeking to shed those extra pounds, or someone simply wanting to boost your overall health, we hope that the knowledge you gain here will empower you to step confidently on the path toward your goals. Welcome to your journey of carb cycling, where flexibility meets nutrition and where our health and well-being take center stage.

CHAPTER 1
Carb Cycling

Changing the proportion of carbohydrates you consume over the course of a predetermined period of time is what "carb cycling" refers to. It is possible that it will help you shed fat while supporting your efforts to reduce weight while maintaining your physical performance.

Consumption of carbohydrates has been a hot issue for a considerable amount of time. There are a few different diets that are effective, and some of them limit or even completely eliminate carbohydrates. However, there is no such thing as an inherently harmful macronutrient, and this includes carbohydrates. Your daily consumption of carbohydrates is something that needs to be adjusted according to who you are as a person.

Some individuals nowadays "cycle" their carbs in order to make adjustments to the total amount of carbohydrates that they consume. Carb cycling is the term for this practice.

This chapter presents a comprehensive analysis of the science behind carb cycling as well as its practical applications.

What is Carb Cycling?

Carb cycling is a method of dieting in which you vary the amount of carbohydrates you consume on a daily, weekly, or monthly basis, respectively.

People utilize it for a variety of reasons, including to cut fat, to keep their physical performance up while dieting, and to break through weight loss plateaus.

Some individuals change their carbohydrate consumption on a daily basis, while others may engage in prolonged periods of low, moderate, or high carbohydrate consumption.

Carb cycling, in a nutshell, involves timing the use of carbohydrates such that they give the most benefit and avoiding them at times when they are not required.

You are able to plan your consumption of carbohydrates according to a range of circumstances, such as:

In order to achieve their body composition objectives, some individuals would limit the amount of carbohydrates they consume when on a diet and then gradually increase the amount of carbohydrates they consume while in a "muscle building" or performance phase.

- Training days and rest days: One common strategy calls for a greater consumption of carbohydrates on training days and a reduced intake of carbohydrates on rest days.
- Scheduled refeeds are still another common method, and they include eating an extremely high amount of carbohydrates for a day or many days as a "refeed" when on a diet for an extended period of time.
- Athletes may often "carb load" in the days leading up to competition, and many physique competitors will do the same thing before a bodybuilding contest or photoshoot.
- Individuals will adjust the quantity of carbohydrates they consume based on the kind of workout they are doing, as well as the intensity and length of the workout. They will consume a greater quantity of carbohydrates in direct proportion to the length and intensity of the workout, and vice versa.
- Body fat levels: Many people will cycle their carbohydrate consumption depending on the degree of body fat that they have. When they become thinner, they will contain more days or blocks that are heavy in carbohydrates.

Two days with a high carbohydrate intake, two days with a moderate carbohydrate intake, and three days with a low carbohydrate intake would make up a typical weekly carb cycling diet.

While the amount of protein consumed is often consistent from day to day, the amount of fat consumed shifts in response to the amount of carbohydrates consumed.

A day that is low in carbs will often be high in fat, whereas days that are heavy in carbs will be low in fat.

Carb cycling is an advanced method of dieting that, in comparison to a regular diet, calls for a greater degree of manipulation and planning. It would be beneficial to get the advice of a trained dietician in order to do this properly.

The Science Behind Carb Cycling

Carb cycling is a method of dieting that was developed very recently.

The primary focus of this field of study is on the biological processes that underlie the modulation of carbohydrates.

Carb-cycling diets have only been the subject of a limited amount of controlled research.

Carb cycling is an effort to meet the requirements for glucose or calories that are set by your body. For instance, it supplies carbs before your exercise or on days when your training is particularly hard.

The days when you consume a lot of carbohydrates also assist your body in restoring its supply of muscle glycogen, which may lead to improved performance and a reduction in muscle breakdown.

Periods of time strategically spent eating a lot of carbohydrates may also increase the function of hormones that regulate hunger and body weight, namely leptin and ghrelin.

It is said that participating in low-carb days causes your body to adapt to an energy system that is mostly fat-based. This may increase your metabolic flexibility and your body's capacity to use fat as fuel over the long run.

The modulation of insulin levels is an additional significant component of carb cycling.

Insulin sensitivity is an important indicator of overall health and low-carb days, and carbohydrate targeting around exercise may help enhance it.

In principle, this strategy might provide support for the advantages that carbs offer.

Because there hasn't been enough actual study done on the topic, it's best to proceed with caution while using this method, despite the fact that the mechanics underlying carb cycling lend credence to its use. To determine if carb cycling is both safe and effective, a significant number of further clinical investigations involving human volunteers are required.

Can Carb Cycling help you Lose Weight?

Carb cycling seems to have processes that are compatible with weight reduction, which is good news for those who are trying to trim their waistlines.

Carb cycling is an approach that, in principle, may help you keep up your physical performance while simultaneously pushing your body to burn fat for fuel. As is the case with many dietary plans, the primary factor in successful weight reduction is the creation of a calorie deficit, which occurs when an individual consumes fewer calories than their body expends over an extended period of time.

If you combine a calorie deficit with a diet that involves cycling different types of carbohydrates, you will most likely see weight loss. On the other hand, due to the intricate nature of carb cycling, newbies may find it challenging to adhere to the plan and avoid becoming confused.

Carb cycling, on the other hand, may be something that many individuals find to be very flexible and enjoyable. For certain individuals, this may boost their ability to stick to the plan and achieve success over the long run.

Carb Cycling for Muscle Growth and sports performance

Carb cycling is one of those diet strategies that many people feel will help them grow muscle and improve their physical performance.

It's possible that the planned carb intake and repeated high-carb periods will boost performance.

Consuming carbohydrates around the time of exercise may also help with recuperation, the transport of nutrients, and the replenishment of glycogen. It's possible that this will stimulate muscular development. However, other studies show that carbohydrates are not required to grow muscle, provided an adequate amount of protein is consumed.

Although, in principle, these processes make sense, in order to give a response that is supported by data, we need a direct study that compares carb cycling to other diets. In addition, the concept that "carb loading" would boost either athletic performance or muscle development is not supported by all of the data. In general, there is not enough information available to know for certain.

The Benefits of Carb Cycling

Lean Muscle Mass growth and retention

Carb cycling is a method that may be used to either lose fat or gain weight. The number of days on which one consumes a low-carb diet is the primary factor that determines whether one has a net calorie deficit or calorie surplus.

You may help your body burn off some of the body fat you may be gaining by including a few low-carb days into your mass-gain program. This will cause lipogenesis to slow down and boost the rate at which your body breaks down fatty acids.

On the other hand, if you include a few high-carb days into your fat reduction regimen, you will create an anabolic environment. This will allow you to perhaps grow some muscle and certainly keep more mass (due to higher amino acid intake, increased protein synthesis, and decreased protein breakdown). In any case, over the course of a week, you will see a simultaneous reduction in body fat and an increase in the amount of muscle you have gained or maintained.

Endocrine Stimulation

It has been well known that maintaining a low-carbohydrate diet for an extended length of time may cause a fall in thyroid hormone levels (T3), which in turn leads to a reduction in Basal Metabolic Rate (the number of calories burned at rest), which makes it harder to break through fat-loss plateaus. Intentional high-carb days will cause an increase in the synthesis of T3, which will speed up your metabolism and make it possible for you to lose even more body fat.

In addition to this, research has shown that a diet low in carbohydrates (with less than thirty percent of total calories coming from carbohydrates) may reduce the ratio of free testosterone to cortisol in as little as three days after intense exercise. You will be able to boost the anabolic-testosterone-to-catabolic-cortisol ratio and welcome back the gains if you intersperse your training with days in which you consume a larger carbohydrate intake.

Overeating carbohydrates may also lead to an increase in leptin levels, often known as the "satiety hormone." This hormone is released at a lower rate in response to reduced fat cell size, which occurs throughout the process of fat reduction. You can expect to feel less hungry for a few days following a day during which you consume a lot of carbohydrates, which will enable you to maintain your trim.

Having a positive mood the day after eating a diet heavy in carbohydrates may be beneficial for both the drive to workout and the adherence to the diet. Insulin may be able to aid with this by increasing the accessibility of tryptophan, which is a precursor to the 'good mood' neurotransmitter known as serotonin in the brain.

Glycogen Super-Compensation

It's possible to dramatically cut down on the quantity of glycogen stored in your muscles by combining a few days of low-carbohydrate eating with intense exercise. This stimulates the creation of an enzyme known as glycogen synthase, which then goes to greater lengths to convert as much glucose as it can into glycogen (which is then stored in the muscles and liver).

After increasing your consumption of carbohydrates, it will take some time for the body to realize that there is a sufficient amount of glucose available for the enzyme to slow down its activity. Meanwhile, your muscles will suck up carbohydrates like sponges, accumulating glycogen at a rate that is higher than their typical capability. This will result in your muscles being fuller, tougher, and larger. When it comes to taking the clothing off for a stage performance or picture session, having this effect happen at the appropriate moment may make a significant difference in how the subject appears.

Hormone Balance

There has been very little study conducted on the relationship between carb cycling and hormones; nonetheless, there is reason to assume that low-carb and keto diets have the ability to promote healthy hormones in many individuals. Eating fewer carbohydrates has been linked to improvements in insulin sensitivity as well as reductions in hyperinsulinemia (high insulin levels). Following a keto-Mediterranean diet was associated with research on women with PCOS—aa disorder characterized by insulin resistance, high testosterone levels, and decreased fertility—with improvements in insulin resistance, lower testosterone levels, and favorable increases in estrogen and progesterone. The study was conducted on individuals who had PCOS.

Having said that, prolonged low-carb and ketogenic diets have the potential to put some people's hormones out of sync. This is especially true for women. Reduced levels of leptin, erratic menstrual cycles, and low levels of T3 (the active thyroid hormone which influences metabolism and body weight) have all been linked to these diets. According to Miller's observations, women who are physically fit, very active, and have high levels of the stress hormone cortisol are often at the greatest risk for developing these hormonal abnormalities. It's possible that this is caused mostly by leptin, which in turn has an effect on other hormones.

The function of the hormone leptin is to send signals about the amount of available energy to the body. It is released by adipose tissue in reaction to rises in blood glucose and insulin, which cause feelings of satiety to occur as a direct consequence of these changes. According to Miller, though, your leptin levels are more likely to be low if you are on a low-carb diet and do not have a significant amount of body fat. This is based on what she observes in her clients. This may lead to feelings of hunger, menstrual cycle irregularities, and even changes in thyroid hormone levels. Restoring appropriate levels of leptin is one of the primary reasons why Miller employs carb cycling with her keto clients. She has shown that this may have a cascade of favorable consequences such as greater satiety (i.e., less hunger), more regular periods, and enhanced fertility.

Microbiome

Carb cycling is a method that may be used to promote the microbiome of the gut, which in turn has a significant influence on metabolic health. The data on the effects of high-fat, low-carb diets on the gut microbiome is inconsistent; nevertheless, some studies show that these diets encourage the development of bacteria that are harmful to the gut and suppress the growth of bacteria that are healthy to the gut. This is probably at least partially attributable to a decrease in the consumption of fiber. The good news is that carb cycling makes it possible to consume more vegetables, fruits, legumes, and other whole-food carbohydrates, all of which are excellent sources of healthy fiber. This increased fiber, in turn, acts as a source of fuel for the good bacteria that are resident in your gut, leading to the synthesis of beneficial substances known as short-chain fatty acids (SCFAs), which assist in the production of hormones that regulate glucose levels.

Consuming a sufficient amount of fiber is essential for not just maintaining a healthy intestinal mucus barrier but also controlling inflammation. In a state in which you are not getting enough fiber, the bacteria in your gut will begin to eat away at the protective mucus layer that lines your intestines. This can lead to a condition known as "leaky gut," in which food particles and toxins enter the bloodstream and promote chronic inflammation. Chronic inflammation is the root cause of a wide variety of metabolic disorders.

Considerations and Precautions

Because there is no specific or scientific definition of carb cycling, many of its purported advantages are based on individual results rather than scientific evidence, and the programs that you see online may vary dramatically depending on who they're targeting. Since there is no exact or scientific definition of carb cycling, many of its purported benefits are based on individual outcomes. Methods designed for individuals who want to enhance their health, for example, are likely to be very different from those designed for those who want to put muscle in their bodies. However, here is the overarching premise: Consume a diet that is low in carbohydrates or follows the ketogenic protocol for most of the time, and then deliberately consume a greater quantity of carbohydrates on certain days (or at precise intervals) to support particular goals.

Consuming a diet low in carbohydrates causes a significant alteration in the metabolism: You will mostly be using fat and ketones for fuel, as opposed to the glucose that comes from carbohydrates. The term "metabolic flexibility" refers to the capacity of the organism to transition between glucose and fat as a source of energy. Consuming carbohydrates at strategic intervals helps replace muscle glycogen (since carbohydrates that aren't immediately utilized as fuel will be stored as glycogen before being stored as fat if glycogen levels are low), and it may also have a positive effect on the release of hormones like leptin.

Carb cycling is a method that functional medicine dietitian and certified diabetes educator Ali Miller, RD, CDE, often employs with her patients and clientele. What she has seen is that periodic carb cycles, also known as windows of consuming higher carbs, can support outcomes with exercise (enhanced endurance and performance), the microbiome (by providing more fiber than traditional low-carb diets), and metabolic hormones among people who typically eat at a lower carbohydrate threshold.

How would anything like this manifest itself in the actual world? Working out while in a state of ketosis or low carbohydrate consumption may provide athletes and fitness enthusiasts with a means to burn a greater proportion of fat (including fat that has been stored) over an extended amount of time. This may help improve body composition, making it easier to achieve a target weight or percentage of body fat. Then, increasing carbohydrate consumption at strategic intervals (for example, around specific athletic events) could help replenish muscle glycogen, which would provide the body with an additional fuel source that is more efficient for high-intensity activities (such as hill sprints and strength training) as well as long-duration competitive events (such as a marathon, triathlon, or bike race).

And according to Miller, taking more carbohydrates at crucial moments in a woman's menstrual cycle may give comfort by boosting levels of leptin, which may help certain women who are on low-carb diets who deal with difficulties such as poor energy, feelings of hunger, and monthly abnormalities. This is especially true for lean, active women who are struggling with these issues.

With carb-cycling, I've seen enhanced exercise endurance and performance, as well as improvements in hormones, as demonstrated by healthy menstrual cycles and a return to ovulation after being anovulatory. I've also seen a return to ovulation after being anovulatory. Also, "I've seen leptin go from being deficient to optimal.

Carb cycling, however, does not have to be restricted to the aforementioned food categories. It's an option for practically anybody who is interested in the advantages of a low-carb or keto diet but desires an approach that is more flexible and minimizes the possible drawbacks of following either of those lifestyles.

What does a Typical Carb Cycle" look like?

There is not a single optimal strategy for carb cycling. The strategy that will work best for you will be determined by the health objectives that you have set for yourself as well as by what feels comfortable, and it will most likely take some trial and error to find the rhythm that works best for you.

For instance, you could carb cycle every week by eating low-carb for six days (5–10% of calories from carbs, or 25–50 g carbs on a 2,000 calorie per day diet, is a popular range*), then eating relatively higher carbs (1.5-2x your low-carb intake) for one day in conjunction with your most strenuous workout or a social event. This could help you maintain your muscle mass and prevent you from gaining weight. Therefore, if you consume 40 grams of carbohydrates on a daily basis, higher carbohydrate days would range from 60 to 80 grams. This does not imply "high" carbs—a large jump in blood sugar is not the aim—but it will be higher than your regular set point. The goal here is to maintain a steady blood sugar level.

If you want to maintain the best possible metabolic health, it is advisable to keep the following recommendations in mind while cycling carbs:

- Choose sources of whole foods that are high in nutrients.
- Steer clear of processed sweets and carbohydrates.
- Whenever it is feasible, give preference to vegetables that are not starchy, such as greens, cabbage, and bell peppers. Consume healthy starchy vegetables and legumes, such as sweet potatoes, carrots, squash, peas, and beans, in only small quantities.
- Put more emphasis on fruits like apples, berries, and citrus fruits because of their high fiber and antioxidant content.
- Consuming meals heavy in carbohydrates should be accompanied by foods high in fat and protein in order to reduce the likelihood of blood glucose levels increasing.

In order to prevent spikes in blood sugar and insulin after eating a meal that is heavy in carbohydrates, go for a walk after the meal (preferably within 30 minutes, although walking at other times of the day may also be beneficial).

Eating a low-carbohydrate diet for six to eight weeks, followed by a week of eating a higher-carbohydrate diet—possibly in combination with a vacation or a more rigorous training block—is another possibility.

On the other hand, Caution against cycling carbohydrate intake too regularly. That's more than once a week for the typical individual, and it's especially important to remember that while you're attempting to go into ketosis. Because it may take many individuals two to three days to enter ketosis, if you carb up too often, you may never get there on your low-carb days. This is especially true if you are trying to lose weight.

One thing to keep in mind is that increasing your consumption of carbohydrates after having been mostly low-carb might possibly upset your stomach. Therefore, rather than increasing the amount of carbohydrates you eat in a single day, you should increase them gradually while monitoring how your body reacts.

CHAPTER 2
The Fundamental of Carb Cycling

fitness goals. This method involves alternating between high-carbohydrate and low-carbohydrate days in a structured manner to optimize nutrient intake and manipulate insulin levels. By strategically adjusting carbohydrate intake, individuals can enhance fat loss, improve athletic performance, and promote overall well-being.

Assessing Your Goals and Needs

Before embarking on any dietary plan, it is vital to establish clear goals. Carb cycling, while versatile, may not be suitable for everyone. Therefore, it is essential to assess your objectives and determine if they align with the potential benefits of carb cycling. Common goals that can be effectively supported by carb cycling include:

Fat Loss

If your primary objective is to shed excess body fat, carb cycling can be an excellent strategy. By manipulating carbohydrate intake, you can create an energy deficit, which promotes fat oxidation and facilitates weight loss. Carb cycling can also help mitigate the metabolic adaptations that often occur with prolonged calorie restriction.

Muscle Gain and Strength

Carb cycling can be a valuable tool for individuals aiming to build muscle and enhance strength. By strategically timing high-carbohydrate days around intense training sessions, you provide your muscles with the necessary fuel to perform optimally. Additionally, adequate carbohydrate intake helps support glycogen replenishment and muscle recovery.

Athletic Performance

Carbohydrates are the body's preferred source of energy during high-intensity exercise. By incorporating carb cycling, athletes can optimize their carbohydrate intake to fuel performance during training and competition. This approach ensures that glycogen stores are adequately replenished while avoiding excessive carbohydrate consumption during periods of lower activity.

Assessing Personal Preferences and Lifestyle Factors

While understanding your goals is crucial, it is equally important to consider your personal preferences and lifestyle factors when evaluating the suitability of carb cycling. Factors to consider include:

Food Preferences

Carb cycling typically involves altering the intake of starchy and sugary carbohydrates. If you have specific dietary restrictions or preferences that limit your carbohydrate choices, it may be challenging to adhere to a carb cycling plan. However, with careful planning and food substitutions, it is possible to tailor a carb-cycling approach that suits your needs.

Meal Timing and Frequency

Carb cycling often requires planning meals and adjusting macronutrient ratios based on training schedules and activity levels. If you prefer a more flexible eating pattern or have irregular work hours, it is essential to determine if carb cycling aligns with your lifestyle and eating preferences.

Social Considerations

Social occasions and events that involve food can present challenges when following a carb-cycling protocol. It is important to assess how carb cycling fits into your social life and consider strategies for navigating these situations while still adhering to your dietary goals.

Health Considerations

Individuals with specific health conditions, such as diabetes or metabolic disorders, should consult with a healthcare professional before adopting a carb-cycling approach. It is crucial to ensure that carbohydrate cycling is safe and appropriate for your individual circumstances.

Determining Your High, Low, and No-Carb Days

High Carb Day

- Breakfast: 3 hard-boiled eggs, 3 pieces of Ezekiel (or 7-seed or grain) bread, tomatoes, mushrooms, and a side of mixed fruit (totaling 60 grams of carbohydrates).
- Lunch: 45 grams of carbohydrates may be obtained by consuming six ounces (oz) each of sweet potatoes, lean meat or fish, and a variety of vegetables.
- Pre-workout: 50 grams of carbohydrates may be found in a single dish of oatmeal, almond milk, one cup of berries, and one scoop of whey protein.
- Dinner: 1 portion of brown rice, 6 ounces of lean chicken, 1 portion of homemade tomato sauce, 1 portion of kidney beans, and a variety of veggies make up the 70 grams of carbohydrates in this meal.

Moderate Carb Day

- Breakfast: A serving of high-protein yogurt, one cup of mixed berries, one teaspoon of seed mix, and 25 grams of total carbohydrates.
- Lunch: 6 ounces of chicken salad combined with 4 ounces of diced potatoes results in 25 grams of carbohydrates.
- Pre-workout: 30 grams of carbohydrates may be found in 1 banana and 1 whey protein smoothie.
- Dinner: 40 grams of carbohydrates may be found in one serving of sweet potato fries, 6 ounces of lean meat, homemade tomato sauce, one dish of kidney beans, and a variety of veggies.

Low Carb Day

- Breakfast: 10 grams of carbohydrates may be found in a serving of three eggs, three pieces of bacon, and a variety of veggies.
- Lunch: 10 grams of carbohydrates may be found in a serving of 6 ounces of salmon salad with 1 teaspoon of olive oil.
- Snack: 1 ounce of mixed nuts and one dish of turkey slices will provide 10 grams of carbohydrates.
- Dinner: 16 grams of carbohydrates may be found in the steak, avocado, and vegetable mixture that is 6 ounces in size.

Recommended Carbohydrate Food Sources

Cakes, sweets, highly processed snack foods, and baked goods are examples of the types of foods that include refined carbohydrates and simple sugars, both of which should be consumed in moderation. Baked goods, cakes, and desserts are also examples of foods that contain complex carbs.

On the other hand, there is an abundance of nutritious sources of carbohydrates that are not only delicious but also rich in important fiber, vitamins, and minerals.

Focus on these more nutritious options for carbohydrates while you're planning your high-carb days.

Recommended Carbs

Instead of classifying different types of carbohydrates as "good" or "bad," you should aim to consume as many unprocessed carbs as you can. These are the following:

- Whole grains: Grains that have not been altered in any way are completely safe to consume and may provide a wide range of additional advantages. Brown rice, oats, and quinoa are a few examples of whole grains.
- Vegetables: The amounts of vitamins and minerals that are included in various vegetables vary greatly. Consume foods that range in hue to achieve nutritional parity.

- Whole fruits: Every kind of fruit has its own distinct characteristics, and berries, in particular, are known for their high antioxidant content and low glycemic load.
- Legumes: These are an excellent source of carbs since they are digested slowly and include a wealth of fiber and minerals.
- Tubers: Potatoes and sweet potatoes are both considered to fall within this group.

Calculating Macronutrient Requirements

It's possible that counting macros can help you lose weight, enhance the overall quality of your diet, and achieve certain health-related objectives faster. It entails figuring out what your nutritional requirements are and keeping a food diary or utilizing an app to keep track of what you consume.

There is a good probability that you are familiar with the phrase "counting macros" if you are a member of a fitness facility or if you are actively involved in the health community.

Counting macronutrients, often known as macros, is a strategy that may assist you in reaching a variety of health objectives. This strategy is commonly employed by those who want to lose weight or develop muscle mass.

It requires maintaining a log of the calories you consume as well as the kinds of meals you consume in order to meet predetermined calorie and macronutrient requirements. Even though counting macros is not a very difficult task, doing it for the first time might be rather overwhelming.

What Are "Micro" Nutrients?

In order to correctly calculate macronutrients, it is crucial to first understand what macronutrients are and the reasons why different individuals need varying proportions of them in their diets.

Carbohydrates

Sugars, starches, and fiber all fall under the category of carbohydrates.

The majority of carbohydrates are metabolized into glucose, often known as sugar. Glucose may either be used by your body for immediate energy or stored as glycogen, which is the form of glucose used for storage in your liver and muscles.

Carbohydrates have a calorie density of four calories per gram (g), making them the primary contributor to the average person's overall calorie consumption.

Carbohydrate consumption is one of the macronutrient recommendations that generate the most controversy; however, most prominent health organizations recommend getting 45–65 percent of your daily calories from carbohydrates. Foods such as grains, vegetables, legumes, dairy products, and fruits all contain carbohydrate content in varying amounts.

Fats

When compared to other macronutrients, fats have the highest caloric density, with 9 calories packed into every single gram of fat.

Fat is essential to the creation of hormones, the absorption of nutrients, and the regulation of your body temperature. It also provides your body with the energy it needs.

Although the normal recommendations for fats as a macronutrient vary from 20%–35% of total calories, many individuals find that following a diet that is higher in fat is successful for them.

Foods like oils, butter, avocado, nuts, seeds, meat, and fish with high-fat content are all good sources of fat.

Proteins

Like carbohydrates, proteins supply 4 calories per gram.

Proteins play an essential role in a wide variety of biological activities, including cell communication, immune system function, and the formation of tissues, hormones, and enzymes.

It is advised that between 10 and 35 percent of your daily caloric intake comes from proteins.

However, suggestions for how much protein you should consume change based on factors such as your age, health, and other factors.

Foods such as meat, eggs, chicken, fish, tofu, and lentils are all examples of foods that are high in protein.

How to Determine the Amount of Macronutrients

Counting macronutrients is a strategy that can be used by anyone, despite the fact that learning how to do so requires some work.

You may get started using the steps that are listed below.

1. Figure Out Your Calorie Requirements.

You have to figure out both your resting energy expenditure (also known as REE) and your non-resting energy expenditure (also known as NREE) in order to calculate your total calorie requirements.

Resting energy expenditure, or REE, is the number of calories burned by a person when at rest, while the number of calories expended during exercise and digestion is shown by NREE.

When you add together your REE and NREE, you will arrive at the total amount of calories expended in a day, which is also referred to as your TDEE (total daily energy expenditure).

You have the option of using a simple online calculator or the Mifflin-St. Jeor equation in order to compute the total number of calories that your body requires on a daily basis.

- Calculate your daily calorie intake by multiplying your weight in kilograms by 10, your height in centimeters by 6.25, and your age in years by 5.
- For women, the number of calories needed per day is calculated as follows: calories = 10 x weight (kg) + 6.25 x height (cm) - 5 x age (years) - 161

After that, multiply your result by an activity factor, which is a value that indicates various intensities of activity:

- Stagnant: x 1.2 (low levels of physical activity)
- Lightly active: multiplied by 1.375 (less than three days of gentle activity per week).
- Moderately active: x 1.55 (moderate exercise most days of the week)
- Extremely active: multiplied by 1.75 (daily strenuous exercise)
- Those who are really active: x 1.9 (strenuous activity at least twice a day)

Your TDEE may then be calculated based on the final result.

In order to accomplish a variety of objectives, you may adjust the overall number of calories you consume by either adding or removing calories.

To put it another way, those who want to reduce their body fat percentage should reduce the number of calories they eat below the amount of energy they spend, but those who wish to grow their muscle mass should take in more calories.

2. Decide Your Optimum Macronutrient Breakdown.

The following stage, after estimating how many calories you should take on a daily basis, is to choose the macronutrient ratio that will be most beneficial to your body.

The following is a list of the typical recommendations for macronutrients:

- 45%–65% of the total calories come from carbohydrates.
- 20%–35% of the total calories come from fat.

- 10%–35% of the total calories come from proteins.

Bear in mind that these suggestions may not work for the demands that you have specifically.

Your ratio is something that may be adjusted to meet a variety of needs and requirements.

For instance, a person who wishes to improve their ability to manage their blood sugar and decrease extra body fat may find success following a diet plan that consists of 35% carbohydrates, 30% fat, and 35% protein.

A person who follows a ketogenic diet would need much greater fat consumption and a lower carbohydrate intake, but an endurance athlete may require a higher carbohydrate intake.

As can be seen, the ratios of macronutrients may change based on dietary choices, the amount of weight one wishes to lose, and a variety of other variables.

3. Keep A Close Eye on Both Your Calorie and Macronutrient Consumption.

After that, it is time to begin keeping track of your macros.

Logging the meals you consume on a website, in an app, or in a food diary is what "tracking macros" refers to in its most basic form.

It's possible that using a nutrition app like MyFitnessPal, Lose It!, or My Macros + is the most time- and effort-efficient method to keep track of your macros.

These applications are easy to use and were developed with the express purpose of making tracking macros easier.

In addition, while it is not required, using a digital food scale might assist you in keeping track of your macronutrient intake. If you decide to get one, be sure to weigh every piece of food that you consume before entering the information into the app of your choosing.

There are a number of applications that come equipped with a barcode scanner that can automatically enter the portion size of the item you scan into your macro log.

In addition to this, you may write macros by hand in a tangible notebook. Your own preferences will determine the approach you use.

It is important to keep in mind that it is not required to precisely reach your macro-objectives. Even if you go a few grams over or under each day, you may still get the results you want.

4. An Illustration of Counting

An example of how to calculate the macronutrients in a diet that consists of 40% carbohydrates, 30% protein, and 30% fat is shown below. This diet has a total calorie intake of 2,000.

Carbs:
- 4 calories per g
- Carbohydrates account for 40% of daily caloric intake or 800 calories.
- Total g of carbs allowed per day = 800/4 = 200 g

Proteins:
- 4 calories per g
- 600 calories per day are equivalent to 30% of 2,000 calories, which is protein.
- The daily maximum amount of permissible protein consumption is equal to 600 g divided by four.

Fats:
- 9 calories per g
- 600 calories per day are equivalent to 30% of 2,000 calories, which is protein.
- The daily limit for total grams of fat is 600 divided by nine, which is 67 grams.
- Your optimum daily intake would consist of 67 grams of fat, 200 grams of carbohydrates, and 150 grams of protein if this were the case.

Benefits

The counting of macronutrients can be beneficial in more ways than one.

Result in An Improved Overall Diet

If you count macros, you may focus your attention on the quality of the food you eat rather than the amount of calories it contains.

For instance, a bowl of sugary cereal may have the same amount of calories as a bowl of oats topped with berries and pumpkin seeds, but the composition of these two breakfasts couldn't be more different in terms of the macronutrients they contain.

In order to stay within the allotted limits for each macronutrient, counting your macros could encourage you to choose meals that are higher in nutrients.

However, meals with a lower nutritional density may still fit within your macros and calorie goals; thus, it is essential to place emphasis on foods with a high nutrient density.

The Reduction of Body Fat

Because it outlines precise dietary guidelines, counting macros may prove to be a very successful method for shedding excess pounds.

For example, those who are following high-protein, low-carbohydrate diets, which have been associated with weight reduction, may benefit from measuring their macros.

In addition, studies have shown that keeping a food journal may assist with the long-term maintenance of a healthy weight.

Could Be of Assistance with Certain Objectives

The practice of calculating macronutrients is common among athletes and anyone whose specialized health objectives extend beyond simple weight reduction.

People who want to increase their muscle mass may have higher requirements for protein than those who merely want to reduce their overall body fat percentage.

Those individuals who need to eat certain quantities of macronutrients in order to improve their performance and acquire lean body mass are the ones who absolutely need to count their macros.

For instance, studies have shown that athletes who engage in resistance training may need as much as 1.4 grams of protein per pound (lb) (3.1 grams per kilogram) of body weight each day in order to preserve their muscle mass.

CHAPTER 3
High-Carb Days: Fueling Performance

Importance of Carbohydrates for Exercise

The digestive system is responsible for converting the macronutrients known as carbohydrates into glucose, often known as blood sugar. Carbohydrates include sugars, starches, and fiber. The glucose then makes its way through the circulatory system and into the cells, where it may either be immediately utilized for energy or stored in our muscles and liver as glycogen, a type of sugar that can be used for fuel at a later time.

Carbohydrates are a vital source of fuel for any type of physical activity, including workouts.

If you engage in physical activity without first consuming carbohydrates — and if you typically do not consume a sufficient quantity of these macronutrients in your diet to have a sizable reserve of glycogen in your muscles — your body will instead break down the protein that is stored in your muscles in order to use it as a source of fuel. During strenuous exercise, tapping into these protein reserves might make you more susceptible to exhaustion, as well as dizziness and dehydration.

Choosing Optimal Carbohydrate Sources

Carbohydrates may be broken down into two categories: simple and complicated. The quantity of sugar molecules that each of these items has is what differentiates them from one another.

Simple Carbohydrates

Simple carbohydrates are those that just have one or two sugar molecules in them and have a very straightforward chemical structure. They are swiftly broken down by the body because of their basic structure; as a result, they provide a source of energy that may be used immediately. However, this may also contribute to spikes and dips in blood sugar, which can cause an increase in appetite.

However, simple carbohydrates are typically the foundation of many highly refined and ultra-processed meals as well. Simple carbs may be found in certain whole foods that are healthful, such as fruits and products made from milk. These include white bread, cookies, sweets, and sodas, all of which are foods that often include a low amount of fiber, a high amount of added sugar, and a lack of essential nutrients. Because of the effect that simple carbohydrates have on one's blood sugar, they are given a high ranking on a scale that is referred to as the "glycemic index." The glycemic index assigns a score between 0 and 100 to each food item depending on how big of an increase in blood sugar levels a specific meal causes two hours after you've eaten it. The greater the score, the more your blood sugar will be raised by eating it. One hundred grams of white bread, for instance, has a value of 73, but one hundred grams of broccoli has a value of 15. This indicates that eating the same quantity of white bread will have a considerably greater effect on elevating your blood sugar than eating the same quantity of broccoli.

Complex Carbohydrates

On the other hand, complex carbohydrates are made up of three or more sugars grouped in a more sophisticated molecular structure. This makes them more difficult to digest. They are metabolized by the body at a more measured pace, resulting in a more gradual effect on overall blood sugar levels. Additionally, complex carbs have the ability to heighten sensations of fullness. This was shown in research that looked at the difference between a meal that had simple carbs and one that contained complex carbohydrates. The researchers showed that eating a lunch that was high in simple carbohydrates led to a significant increase in blood sugar, insulin, and triglyceride levels when compared to eating a breakfast that was high in complex carbohydrates. Those individuals who ate the breakfast that included simple carbohydrates reported feeling hungry and exhausted only 90 minutes after eating, while those individuals who ingested the meal that contained complex carbohydrates had greater energy and felt fuller for a longer period of time.

Beans and other legumes, vegetables, certain fruits, and grains in their entire form are all good sources of complex carbs. These foods are not only an abundant supply of vitamins, minerals, and phytonutrients, but they are also an outstanding source of dietary fiber. Fiber has been associated with a decreased risk of various chronic health issues such as heart disease and type 2 diabetes. This is in addition to the fact that fiber makes you feel fuller for longer, which may help you avoid snacking between meals.

Strategies for Timing Carbohydrates

If you are an average, healthy person, you should consume some carbohydrates with each of your meals throughout the day. Carbohydrates are found in the majority of foods and dietary categories; thus, you need to find the proper balance.

However, taking carbohydrates earlier in the day may be preferable if you have the following conditions:

- Want to lose weight or improve blood sugar levels: Because the majority of people in the United States are more active in the morning and more inactive in the evening, eating the majority of your carbohydrates in the evening might induce a surge in blood sugar. The glucose that is not used for energy but is still present in your bloodstream is subsequently stored as fat by your body.

- Exercise in the morning: It is OK to exercise on an empty stomach and enter the fat-burning zone if your morning workout lasts less than an hour. This will help you burn more fat. On the other hand, if you are more of an endurance athlete or if your exercise will last longer than an hour, you should probably have a little snack before you begin. In any scenario, having carbohydrates on hand to help you refuel after your workout is a smart idea.

- Have trouble sleeping: If you go to bed while your meal is still digesting after eating carbohydrates for supper, it may disrupt your sleep. This is particularly true for those who suffer from heartburn. Consuming the appropriate kinds of carbohydrates is necessary in order to get the advantages of having your energy needs met. Consuming meals that are high in sugar and processed might cause your blood sugar to rise rapidly. As a consequence of this, you can start to feel hungry only one to two hours later, at which point you might eat even more. The same thing might happen if you solely consume carbohydrates and do not consume sufficient amounts of protein and fat.

CHAPTER 4
Low-Carb Days: Promoting Fat Loss

A diet that is low in carbohydrates, often known as carbs, restricts the consumption of carbohydrates, such as those that are found in grains, starchy vegetables, and fruit. A diet that is low in carbohydrates places an emphasis on meals that are rich in protein and fat. There are a variety of low-carb diets to choose from. The kinds and amounts of carbohydrates that are permitted to be consumed are restricted in different ways by each diet.

The Role of Low-Carb Days in Fat Loss

In order to successfully lose weight, most people turn to low-carb diets. Some low-carb diets may provide additional health advantages, such as a reduced chance of developing type 2 diabetes and metabolic syndrome, in addition to their ability to aid in weight reduction.

Why you follow a low-carb diet:

You might make the decision to adhere to a low-carb diet because you:

- If you want to reduce weight, you should follow a diet that cuts down on carbohydrates.
- Do you want to make general changes to the way you eat?
- Take pleasure in consuming the types and quantities of food that are allowed on low-carb diets.

Before beginning any program to lose weight, you should first consult with your primary care physician, particularly if you have a preexisting medical condition such as diabetes or heart disease.

Diet Details

The quantity of carbs you consume is restricted when you follow a low-carb diet. There are three categories of carbs:

- Simple and naturally occurring, such as the lactose and fructose found in milk and fruit, respectively.
- Simple and refined, like the sugar that you put on your table.
- Having a high degree of complexity, such as whole grains or beans.
- Complex things that have been simplified, like white flour.

The following are examples of common natural sources of carbohydrates:

- Grains.
- Fruits.
- Vegetables.
- Milk.
- Nuts.
- Seeds.
- Legume crops include common foods like beans, lentils, and peas.

Complex carbohydrates, in general, are digested at a slower rate. In addition, complex carbohydrates have a smaller impact on the amount of sugar that is absorbed into the blood. Additionally, they provide fiber.

Sugar and white flour are examples of refined carbohydrates that are often added to processed meals. White bread and spaghetti, cookies, cake, candy, and sugar-sweetened sodas and beverages are all examples of foods that include refined carbohydrates. Other examples include items like cake and candy.

Carbohydrates are the primary source of fuel for the body. Simple sugars, often known as glucose, are produced from the metabolism of complex carbohydrates, and these sugars are then absorbed into the bloodstream. This is referred to as glucose in the blood.

Insulin is secreted to assist glucose in entering the cells of the body, where it may then be utilized as a source of energy. The liver and the muscles both have the ability to retain excess glucose. Some of it gets converted into fat stores.

A diet that is low in carbohydrates is intended to force the body to utilize its existing fat stores as a source of energy, which ultimately results in weight reduction.

Results

Weight loss

If they reduce their caloric intake and increase the amount of physical exercise they get, most individuals can successfully lose weight. You need to cut your daily caloric intake by between 500 and 750 calories if you want to shed one to one and a half pounds (0.5 to 0.7 kg) each week.

When it comes to weight reduction in the short term, a low-carb diet, particularly a very low-carb diet, may be more effective than a low-fat diet. However, the majority of research has come to the conclusion that beyond 12 or 24 months, the advantages of following a low-carb diet are not particularly significant.

There is a possibility that reducing calories and carbohydrate intake is not the sole factor contributing to weight reduction with low-carb diets. According to a number of studies, increasing the amount of protein and fat in your diet may assist in weight loss by making you feel full for longer. A prolonged feeling of fullness might help you consume less food.

Other Benefits

Diets that are low in carbohydrates and place an emphasis on the consumption of healthy sources of carbohydrates, fat, and protein have the potential to reduce the risk of developing type 2 diabetes and cardiovascular disease. In point of fact, it is possible that your blood sugar and cholesterol levels will improve on practically any diet that assists you in losing extra weight, at least in the short term.

Risks

A sudden and significant reduction in carbohydrate consumption might bring on a variety of unpleasant symptoms in the near term, including the following:

- Constipation.
- Headache.
- Muscle cramping.

Carbohydrate restriction of a severe kind might prompt your body to produce ketones for fuel by breaking down fat stores. This state is referred to as ketosis. Ketosis is associated with a number of adverse symptoms, including poor breath, headache, weakness, and weariness.

It is not quite apparent what kinds of potential dangers to one's health a low-carb diet may bring over the long run. If you cut down on carbohydrates for an extended period of time, you run the risk of depleting your body of certain vitamins and minerals and experiencing digestive problems as a result.

If you consume a diet high in animal fat and protein, you may be increasing your chance of developing cardiovascular disease and some malignancies, according to the opinions of certain professionals in the field of public health.

Consider your options carefully when it comes to the types of fats and proteins before committing to a low-carb diet. Reduce your intake of foods that are rich in saturated and trans fats, such as high-fat meat and dairy products. Consuming any of these meals may increase the likelihood that you may get heart disease.

Selecting Low-Carb Foods

In general, a low-carb diet places an emphasis on proteins and some vegetables that are low in starch. A diet low in carbohydrates often restricts the consumption of grains, legumes, fruits, bread, sweets, pasta, and starchy vegetables, and on occasion, nuts and seeds as well. However, there are low-carb diet programs that still include eating certain fruits, vegetables, and whole grains in moderate quantities.

A low-carb diet often places a cap on the amount of carbs that may be consumed in one day between 0.7 and 2 ounces (20 and 57 grams). The range of calories provided by these quantities of carbs is from 80 to 240. In the first stages of certain low-carb diets, carbohydrate consumption is severely restricted. After a while, such diets start to permit a greater intake of carbohydrates.

On the other hand, the Dietary Guidelines for Americans suggest that carbohydrates should make up between 45% and 65% of one's total daily calorie consumption. If you consume 2,000 calories per day from food and drink, then carbohydrates would account for between 900 and 1,300 of those calories.

Tips for Managing Hunger and Cravings

It's time to visit the 4 Rs: Replenish, Rehydrate, Redirect, and Relax when emotions of hunger — or what feels like hunger — develop when you can't identify the source. Replenishment, rehydration, redirection, and relaxation.

- Replenish: Your first order of business should be to cut down on carbohydrates while simultaneously increasing your intake of protein, fat, and fiber at each meal. If you are doing this regularly, but you are still finding that you are hungry in between meals, you may want to think about taking a multivitamin that also contains minerals. Even a high-quality low-carb diet may, on occasion, not provide sufficient amounts of some necessary elements. There is a need for further study, but some studies show that taking a multivitamin on a regular basis might assist in curbing your hunger and make it simpler to shed unwanted pounds.

- Rehydrate: Is it possible that your body is trying to inform you that it needs water instead of food? It is possible that there may be instances when you are unable to differentiate between thirst and hunger. If you have just finished a meal that was rich in protein, fat, and fiber but you are still hungry, you may want to consider drinking a glass of water, a cup of tea, or another beverage that is low in carbohydrates.
- Redirect: If you've just eaten a meal that's good for you, but you still feel hungry an hour or so later, consider shifting your attention to something else. Put all of your attention on completing the activities at your workplace or around the home. Talk to a buddy on the phone or offer to assist them with a project they are working on. In a nutshell, you should occupy your mind with anything else until the next meal so that you don't dwell on food.
- Relax: It is common to have cravings now and again, as well as feelings of hunger. Even though they happen far less often on a keto or low-carb diet, they may still happen – regardless of whether you are new to this way of eating or have been following it for a while. This is true whether you are following a keto or low-carb diet. Spending some time thinking about these emotions of hunger might help you figure out what's causing them in the first place. On other days, though, you could just feel like eating a little bit more than usual, and that's perfectly OK. Try not to be too critical of yourself. Simply do your best to give your body what it needs when you are, in fact, hungry, enjoy the sensation of eating, and stop when you feel like you have had enough.

CHAPTER 5
No-Carb and Very Low-Carb Days: Enhancing Ketosis and Insulin Sensitivity

The metabolic state known as ketosis takes place when fat rather than glucose is used by the body for energy. Your body's primary source of energy is normal glucose, which is derived from blood sugar.

Consuming foods that are high in carbohydrates (often known as "carbs"), such as starches and sugars, is the most common way to receive glucose from your diet. Your body converts the glucose that it obtains from the breakdown of carbs into its primary source of fuel. The remainder is stored in your liver, which then makes it available as required.

These glucose reserves start to run low when you consume a relatively small amount of carbohydrates. Because there are not enough carbohydrates for your body to use as a source of energy, it will instead burn fat. Ketones are a kind of molecule that is produced whenever fat is broken down in the body. The ketones, also known as ketone bodies, turn out to be the primary source of energy for both the body and the brain.

The fat that your body utilizes to make ketones might come from the food you consume (a process known as nutritional ketosis), or it could come from the fat reserves in your body. Your liver is responsible for the production of a small quantity of ketones on its own. However, when there is a drop in your blood glucose level, there is also a drop in your insulin level. This triggers an increase in the creation of ketones by your liver, which helps to guarantee that it can provide your brain with the necessary amount of energy. As a result, while you are in a state of ketosis, there are significant quantities of ketones in your blood.

What is the Ketosis Diet?

The ketogenic diet, often known as the keto diet, alters the method by which your body processes food. The majority of the fuel that your body requires comes from the carbs that you consume in your diet. The ketogenic diet requires you to consume fewer carbohydrates and instructs your body to shift its fuel source to fat rather than glucose.

The ketogenic diet has a high intake of fat, a moderate amount of protein, and a significant reduction in carbs. A typical ketogenic diet will include 10% to 20% of calories coming from protein, 70% to 80% of calories coming from fat, and 5% to 10% of calories coming from carbs.

There are a lot of meals that are high in nutrients but also include a lot of carbs. This includes foods such as fruits and vegetables, as well as whole grains. On the keto diet, you must limit your consumption of carbohydrates from all sources. As a result, you won't be able to eat any bread, cereal, or other grains, and you'll also have to drastically reduce the amount of fruit and vegetables you consume. The following categories of foods are examples of those that are allowed on the ketogenic diet:

- Meats, as well as fish.
- Eggs.
- Seeds and nuts both
- Buttered cream, if you will.
- Cheese.
- Various kinds of oils, including olive oil and canola oil,

How Many Carbs Do I Need for Ketosis?

In order to enter and remain in ketosis, you will need to keep your daily carbohydrate intake below 50 grams. That's equivalent to around one cup of spaghetti, three pieces of bread, or two bananas.

How Long Does It Take to Get into Ketosis?

If you consume anywhere from 20 to 50 grams of carbs on a daily basis, it will typically take you anywhere from two to four days for your body to go into ketosis. However, the amount of time it takes to reach this condition might vary widely depending on a number of different circumstances. It might take you a week or perhaps longer for your body to go into ketosis. The amount of time it takes you to reach this condition may be affected by a number of factors, including your:

- Age
- Consumption of carbohydrates, fats, and proteins.
- The extent of one's physical activity
- Metabolism.
- Getting enough rest is healthy.
- Stress level

If you follow a diet that is high in carbohydrates before beginning the ketogenic diet, it is possible that it will take you longer to enter the state of ketosis than it would for someone who follows a diet that is low in carbohydrates. This is due to the fact that your body must first use up all of its glucose reserves.

Through intermittent fasting, you could be able to enter ketosis more quickly. Eating all of your meals within a window of eight hours is the approach to intermittent fasting that is practiced the most often. The remaining 16 hours of the 24-hour period are spent abstaining from food and drinking.

What are the Benefits of Ketosis?

According to the findings of several studies, the metabolic state of ketosis may provide a number of health advantages. It is possible that one of the most significant effects of ketosis is weight reduction. The procedure could make you feel less hungry, which in turn might cause you to consume less food overall. It may assist you in losing abdominal fat, also known as visceral fat, while allowing you to keep your lean body mass. Ketosis may also be beneficial in the diagnosis, treatment, and management of disorders such as the following:

- The ketogenic diet is often prescribed to epileptic children by medical professionals in order to modify the "excitability" of a portion of their brains in order to minimize or even eliminate epileptic episodes.
- Research has revealed that following a ketogenic diet may help treat neurological diseases such as Alzheimer's disease, autism and brain malignancies such as glioblastoma.
- People who have type 2 diabetes may find success with the ketogenic diet in terms of both weight loss and better control of their blood sugar levels.
- The ketogenic diet may reduce your chance of developing cardiovascular disease by reducing your blood pressure, boosting your HDL ("good") cholesterol levels, and lowering your triglyceride levels. Heart disease is the most common kind of cardiovascular disease.
- Your chance of acquiring metabolic syndrome, which is connected with your risk of getting heart disease, may be reduced if you follow a ketogenic diet.

It has also been established that entering ketosis might boost your attention as well as your energy levels. Your body will get the energy it needs in a form that is anti-inflammatory when you follow the keto diet. According to research, your brain operates more effectively when it's fed ketones rather than glucose.

Implementing No-Carb and Very Low-Carb Days

Implementing no-carb and very low-carb days is a key aspect of carb cycling. These specific days are designed to manipulate carbohydrate intake and maximize the benefits of the carb-cycling approach. By strategically incorporating periods of extremely low carbohydrate consumption, individuals can enhance fat loss, improve insulin sensitivity, and optimize metabolic flexibility. In this section, we will explore the implementation of no-carb and very low-carb days, including their benefits, considerations, and guidelines for effective execution.

Benefits of No-Carb and Very Low-Carb Days

No-carb and very low-carb days offer several benefits when incorporated into a carb cycling protocol:

1. Enhanced Fat Loss: By significantly reducing carbohydrate intake, these days, we promote a state of ketosis, where the body utilizes fat as its primary source of energy. This can lead to increased fat burning and accelerated fat loss.

2. Improved Insulin Sensitivity: Restricting carbohydrates can improve insulin sensitivity, allowing for better blood sugar control and a reduced risk of insulin resistance and metabolic disorders.

3. Metabolic Flexibility: By cycling between periods of low and higher carbohydrate intake, the body becomes more efficient at utilizing both carbohydrates and fats for energy, enhancing metabolic flexibility.

4. Appetite Control: Lowering carbohydrate intake can help regulate appetite and reduce cravings, leading to improved adherence to the overall dietary plan.

Guidelines for Implementing No-Carb and Very Low-Carb Days

While no-carb and very low-carb days can be effective, it is crucial to approach them with careful planning and consideration. Here are some guidelines to follow when implementing these:

1. Determine the Ideal Macronutrient Ratio: On no-carb and very low-carb days, the primary focus is on minimizing carbohydrate intake. Instead, the majority of calories should come from protein and fat sources. A typical macronutrient ratio for very low-carb days is around 5–10% of calories from carbohydrates, 30–40% from protein, and 50–60% from healthy fats.

2. Choose Suitable Foods: Selecting the right foods is crucial to ensuring adequate nutrient intake and supporting overall health. Opt for whole, unprocessed foods that are low in carbohydrates but rich in essential nutrients. Include lean protein sources, such as chicken, turkey, fish, and tofu, as well as healthy fats from sources like avocados, olive oil, nuts, and seeds.

3. Focus on Non-Starchy Vegetables: Non-starchy vegetables should be a staple on no-carb and very low-carb days. These vegetables are low in carbohydrates and high in fiber, providing essential vitamins and minerals. Examples of non-starchy vegetables include leafy greens, broccoli, cauliflower, zucchini, bell peppers, and asparagus.

4. Plan Meals in Advance: To ensure adherence and success on no-carb and very low-carb days, it is essential to plan meals in advance. This involves preparing meals and snacks that align with the macronutrient ratios and food choices for these specific days. Preparing meals in advance can help avoid impulsive food choices and facilitate adherence to the dietary plan.

5. Stay Hydrated: Adequate hydration is essential during no-carb and very low-carb days. Drink plenty of water throughout the day to support digestion, metabolism, and overall well-being. Herbal teas and infused water can add variety and flavor without adding carbohydrates.

6. Monitor and Adjust: Regularly monitor your progress and make adjustments as needed. Everyone's body responds differently to no-carb and very low-carb days, so pay attention to energy levels, hunger cues, and overall well-being. If necessary, adjust macronutrient ratios, food choices, or the frequency of these days to find the approach that works best for you.

Suitable Foods for No-Carb and Very Low-Carb Days

When implementing no-carb and very low-carb days as part of a carb cycling approach, it is crucial to select foods that are low in carbohydrates but still provide essential nutrients, healthy fats, and adequate protein. These foods will help support overall health, maintain satiety, and ensure a well-rounded nutritional intake. In this section, we will explore suitable food options for no-carb and very low-carb days, providing a variety of choices across different food groups.

Lean Protein Sources

Including lean protein sources is vital on no-carb and very low-carb days to support muscle maintenance, repair, and overall satiety. Opt for the following protein sources:

- Chicken breast
- Turkey breast
- Fish (such as salmon, tuna, trout, and cod)

- Shellfish (such as shrimp, crab, and lobster)
- Lean cuts of beef or pork
- Tofu
- Tempeh
- Eggs
- Greek yogurt (unsweetened and low in carbs)

Healthy Fats

Adding healthy fats to your meals on no-carb and very low-carb days is essential for providing energy, promoting satiety, and supporting various physiological functions. Opt for the following sources of healthy fats:

- Avocado
- Olive oil
- Coconut oil
- Nuts (such as almonds, walnuts, and macadamia nuts)
- Seeds (such as chia seeds, flaxseeds, and pumpkin seeds)
- Nut butter (without added sugars)
- Full-fat cheese (in moderation)

Non-Starchy Vegetables

Non-starchy vegetables are low in carbohydrates and high in fiber, making them excellent choices for no-carb and very low-carb days. These vegetables provide essential vitamins, minerals, and antioxidants. Include a variety of non-starchy vegetables, such as:

- Leafy greens (such as spinach, kale, and arugula)
- Broccoli
- Cauliflower
- Zucchini
- Bell peppers
- Asparagus
- Cucumber
- Brussels sprouts
- Green beans
- Celery
- Mushrooms

Herbs and Spices

Herbs and spices can enhance the flavor of your meals without adding significant carbohydrates. Experiment with different herbs and spices to add variety and enhance the taste of your dishes. Some options include:

- Basil
- Oregano
- Thyme
- Rosemary
- Cilantro
- Parsley
- Cumin
- Turmeric
- Garlic
- Ginger
- Chili powder

Beverages

Staying hydrated is crucial during no-carb and very low-carb days. Opt for zero-calorie or low-calorie beverages that do not contain carbohydrates. Suitable options include:

- Water (plain or infused with lemon, cucumber, or mint)
- Unsweetened herbal teas (such as chamomile, green tea, or peppermint tea)
- Black coffee (without added sugars or creamers)

Supplemental Options

In some cases, individuals may choose to incorporate nutritional supplements to support their dietary needs on no-carb and very low-carb days. Consult with a healthcare professional or registered dietitian before incorporating any supplements. Some options to consider include:

- Whey protein powder (low in carbohydrates and rich in protein)
- Plant-based protein powder (low in carbohydrates and suitable for vegetarians and vegans)
- Omega-3 fish oil capsules (to support healthy fat intake)
- Multivitamin or mineral supplements (to ensure micronutrient needs are met)

Strategies for Transitioning into and Out of Ketosis

Supposedly, you've been on the ketogenic diet for a few months at this point. You have successfully entered ketosis, dropped some weight, and (hopefully) experienced the incredible mental clarity that keto-enthusiasts gush about.

But how do you get your body back to eating regularly after months of eating a diet that is rich in fat, high in protein, and has very little carbohydrates?

When you first started the keto diet, it probably took you a few days to get into ketosis. Therefore, if you suddenly increase the amount of carbohydrates and sugar in your diet, it might wreak havoc on your body and throw it out of ketosis.

If you do not properly transition off of the ketogenic diet, you may be setting yourself up for certain symptoms that are not very attractive, including the following:

- Put on some weight.
- Constipation and other problems related to the restroom.
- Increases in blood sugar may lead to feelings of weariness and irritation in some people.
- A greater need to eat and an addiction to sweets.

Instead, you should use the three strategies outlined below for successfully transitioning off of the ketogenic diet.

1. Focus on Hard to Digest Carbs

After a period of time during which you severely restrict your carbohydrate intake, you should prioritize the consumption of carbohydrates that are rich in both protein and fiber.

If you want to reintroduce carbohydrates into your diet, some terrific possibilities are crackers with seeds, sprouted bread, and spaghetti made from beans. You may also begin to include cashews and avocados in your diet, which are also wonderful additions.

There is a good reason why the abbreviation "carbs" stands for "carbohydrates." Due to the high-water content of these foods, you are likely to see some natural weight gain after reintroducing them into your diet. The important thing is to choose whole-grain carbohydrates that are healthful and won't send your blood sugar levels skyrocketing. Going completely off the rails and starting to consume sweets like doughnuts and cookies is the worst thing you could ever do to yourself. Instead, you should concentrate on the quality of the carbohydrates you eat and choose those that need more time to digest.

The process of withdrawing from the ketogenic diet should take many weeks. It should take your body about a week and a half, at the very most, to acclimatize to the new routine. Some individuals find it useful to increase the amount of carbohydrates they consume on a daily basis by around 10 percent, while others find it helpful to utilize an app to assist in keeping track of their consumption. The most straightforward approach is to pay attention to serving sizes and strive to consume two more portions of carbohydrates on a daily basis.

2. Be Aware of The Sugar Pitfall

Don't replace your ketogenic diet's fat bombs with sugar bombs! One of the advantages of following a ketogenic diet is reducing the amount of sugar you eat and taking out any added sugar from your diet.

If you followed the keto diet for at least a couple of months, you undoubtedly noticed a reduction in your desire for sugary foods. There is scientific evidence demonstrating that sugar is addictive, so why would you want to return to it?

Avoid eating anything that has more than 4 grams of added sugar since this is a good general guideline to follow. Be wary of consuming excessive amounts of naturally occurring sugar, which may sneak up on you in places like honey and some fruits.

Even if all of the sugar in a bar comes from dates, if it contains 22 grams of sugar, that bar is still unhealthy, and you are going to experience a rise in your blood sugar.

3. Good Habits Help

When you began the keto diet for the first time, it undoubtedly took some time for you to educate yourself and learn about the diet. Leaving the keto diet should thus be a gradual and comparable procedure.

Because your surroundings, support system, and lifestyle all play a role in weight reduction, after the keto diet is complete and those things aren't aligned appropriately, it's going to be simple to slip back into old habits and regain the weight that you lost.

When it comes to focusing on good behaviors after the keto diet, staying hydrated is another crucial element. Irritability and the sensation that you are hungry when you are really only thirsty are also side effects of being dehydrated.

It all comes down to picking meals and snacks that are nutritious and well-balanced. Even if you have gained the weight back, it is still possible to lose weight if you focus on consuming nutritious fats, lean proteins, and high-quality carbohydrates.

CHAPTER 6
Recipes

Breakfast Low Carb

1. Sunrise Spinach and Egg Muffins

Preparation Time	Cook Time	Serving Size
15 minutes	20 minutes	Makes 4 muffins (2 per person)

INGREDIENTS:

» 4 large fresh eggs
» 1 cup of finely chopped fresh spinach
» 1/4 cup of finely chopped red bell pepper
» 1/4 cup of finely chopped onion
» 1/4 teaspoon of salt
» 1/4 teaspoon of freshly ground black pepper
» 2 tablespoons of shredded cheddar cheese

INSTRUCTIONS:

1. Preheat your oven to 350°F (175°C). Grease a standard non-stick muffin tin or use silicone muffin cups.
2. In a medium bowl, whisk the eggs until the yolks and whites are fully combined. Stir in the chopped spinach, bell pepper, and onion. Season with salt and black pepper.
3. Evenly distribute the egg and vegetable mixture into the prepared muffin tin, filling each cup about two-thirds full.
4. Sprinkle the shredded cheddar cheese on top of each muffin cup.
5. Bake in the preheated oven for about 20 minutes or until the muffins are set in the center and the cheese is golden and bubbly.
6. Allow the muffins to cool in the pan for a few minutes, then use a butter knife to loosen the edges. Serve warm.

Nutritional Facts (per serving): Calories: 200; Protein: 12g; Fat: 14g; Carbohydrates: 5g; Fiber: 1g.

Tips: To make sure your muffins turn out perfect, avoid overfilling the muffin cups, as the egg will rise as it bakes. Also, let your muffins cool before trying to remove them from the tin; they'll be easier to take out and will hold their shape better. For a healthier twist, you could replace the cheddar with a lower-fat cheese or increase the number of veggies.

2. Avocado Stuffed Omelet

Preparation Time	Cooking Time	Serving Size
10 minutes	15 minutes	Serves 2

INGREDIENTS:

» 4 large eggs
» 1 ripe avocado, pitted and sliced
» 1/4 cup of finely chopped green bell pepper
» 1/4 cup of finely chopped onion
» 1/4 cup of shredded cheddar cheese
» Salt and pepper to taste
» 2 teaspoons of olive oil

INSTRUCTIONS:

1. Crack the eggs into a bowl, season with salt and pepper, and whisk until well mixed.
2. Heat 1 teaspoon of olive oil in a non-stick frying pan over medium heat. Add the onions and bell peppers, sautéing until they're softened and lightly golden.
3. Pour the whisked eggs into the pan, allowing them to spread out evenly over the onions and bell peppers.
4. Arrange the sliced avocado evenly over the top of the egg mixture, and sprinkle with the shredded cheddar cheese.
5. Cover the pan and let cook on medium-low heat until the eggs are fully set and the cheese has melted, about 5 to 7 minutes.
6. Carefully fold the omelet in half using a spatula, then divide it onto two plates. Serve immediately while it's warm.

Nutritional Facts (per serving): Calories: 350; Protein: 15g; Fat: 28g; Carbohydrates: 10g; Fiber: 7g.

Tips: Cook the omelet on medium-low heat to ensure it doesn't burn while it's setting. For added flavor, consider adding fresh herbs like cilantro or parsley, or a dash of hot sauce for some heat.

3. Zesty Zucchini Frittata

Preparation Time	Cooking Time	Serving Size
10 minutes	20 minutes	Serves 2

INGREDIENTS:

» 4 large eggs
» 1 medium zucchini, sliced into thin rounds
» 1/4 cup of finely chopped red onion
» 1/4 teaspoon of crushed red pepper flakes
» Salt and pepper to taste
» 2 tablespoons of grated Parmesan cheese
» 2 teaspoons of olive oil

INSTRUCTIONS:

1. Preheat your oven to 350°F (175°C).
2. In a bowl, whisk the eggs, then season them with the crushed red pepper flakes, salt, and pepper.
3. Heat the olive oil in an oven-safe skillet over medium heat. Add the red onion, cooking until it's softened and translucent.
4. Add the zucchini to the skillet and cook until it's tender, about 5 minutes.
5. Pour the seasoned eggs over the zucchini and onion in the skillet, making sure the mixture is spread evenly.
6. Sprinkle the grated Parmesan cheese over the top of the egg mixture.
7. Place the skillet in the preheated oven and bake for about 10 to 12 minutes, until the frittata is set and lightly golden.
8. Allow the frittata to cool for a few minutes before slicing it into quarters. Serve warm.

Nutritional Facts (per serving): Calories: 280; Protein: 16g; Fat: 20g; Carbohydrates: 6g; Fiber: 1g.

Tips: Make sure to slice the zucchini thinly so that it cooks quickly and evenly. To check if the frittata is ready, you can insert a knife into the center - if it comes out clean, the frittata is done.

4. Keto-Friendly Pancakes

Preparation Time	Cooking Time	Serving Size
10 minutes	15 minutes	Serves 2 (2 pancakes per person)

INGREDIENTS:

» 1/2 cup almond flour
» 2 large eggs
» 2 oz cream cheese, softened
» 1/2 teaspoon baking powder
» 1/4 teaspoon vanilla extract
» A pinch of salt
» 2 tablespoons unsalted butter for frying
» Sugar-free maple syrup, for serving

INSTRUCTIONS:

1. In a blender, combine the almond flour, eggs, cream cheese, baking powder, vanilla extract, and salt. Blend until the mixture is smooth and well combined.
2. Heat a tablespoon of butter in a non-stick skillet over medium heat.
3. Pour a quarter of the pancake batter into the skillet. Cook until you see bubbles form on the surface, about 2-3 minutes. Flip and cook on the other side until golden brown, another 2-3 minutes.
4. Repeat the process with the remaining batter.
5. Serve the pancakes warm with a drizzle of sugar-free maple syrup.

Nutritional Facts (per serving): Calories: 360; Protein: 12g; Fat: 31g; Carbohydrates: 7g (net); Fiber: 3g.

Tips: For an even more decadent breakfast, consider serving these pancakes with a dollop of whipped cream or fresh berries on top. Remember, the batter should be slightly thick - if it's too runny, add a bit more almond flour.

5. Almond Flour Breakfast Biscuits

Preparation Time	Cooking Time	Serving Size
10 minutes	15 minutes	Serves 2 (2 biscuits per person)

INGREDIENTS:

» 1 cup almond flour
» 1 teaspoon baking powder
» 1/4 teaspoon salt
» 2 tablespoons cold unsalted butter, cut into small pieces
» 2 large eggs

INSTRUCTIONS:

1. Preheat your oven to 350°F (175°C). Line a baking sheet with parchment paper.
2. In a bowl, combine the almond flour, baking powder, and salt.
3. Cut in the cold butter with a pastry blender or your fingers until the mixture resembles coarse crumbs.
4. Beat one egg and mix it into the almond flour mixture until a dough forms.
5. Divide the dough into four equal parts, then shape each into a round biscuit on the prepared baking sheet.
6. Beat the second egg and brush it over the tops of the biscuits.
7. Bake in the preheated oven for about 15 minutes, or until the biscuits are golden brown.

Nutritional Facts (per serving): Calories: 350; Protein: 14g; Fat: 31g; Carbohydrates: 8g (net); Fiber: 4g.

Tips: To get flaky, tender biscuits, avoid overworking the dough. Using cold butter also helps achieve this texture. These biscuits pair wonderfully with scrambled eggs or a pat of butter.

6. Smoky Salmon and Cream Cheese Wrap

Preparation Time	Cooking Time	Serving Size
10 minutes	No cook time	Serves 2 (1 wrap per person)

INGREDIENTS:

» 2 low-carb tortilla wraps
» 4 oz smoked salmon
» 1/4 cup cream cheese
» 1 small cucumber, thinly sliced
» 1 small red onion, thinly sliced
» 1 tablespoon chopped fresh dill
» Salt and pepper to taste

INSTRUCTIONS:

1. Lay the low-carb tortillas flat on a clean work surface.
2. Spread half of the cream cheese evenly over each tortilla.
3. Arrange the smoked salmon, cucumber slices, and red onion slices on top of the cream cheese on each tortilla.
4. Sprinkle the fresh dill over the top, then season with a little salt and pepper.
5. Roll each tortilla tightly, being careful to keep the ingredients inside.
6. Slice each wrap in half diagonally before serving.

Nutritional Facts (per serving): Calories: 280; Protein: 18g; Fat: 18g; Carbohydrates: 8g (net); Fiber: 2g.

Tips: For a bit of added tang, consider adding a squeeze of fresh lemon juice over the salmon before rolling the wrap. The wraps can be made ahead of time and stored in the fridge for a quick breakfast on the go.

7. Low Carb Breakfast Burrito

Preparation Time	Cooking Time	Serving Size
10 minutes	15 minutes	Serves 2 (1 burrito per person)

INGREDIENTS:

- » 2 low-carb tortilla wraps
- » 4 large eggs
- » 1/4 cup shredded cheddar cheese
- » 1/4 cup diced bell pepper
- » 1/4 cup diced onion
- » 1/4 cup cooked and crumbled sausage
- » 1 tablespoon olive oil
- » Salt and pepper to taste
- » 1/4 cup salsa, for serving

INSTRUCTIONS:

1. Heat the olive oil in a skillet over medium heat. Add the bell pepper and onion, sautéing until they're softened and slightly caramelized.
2. In a bowl, whisk the eggs, then pour them into the skillet with the sautéed vegetables.
3. Cook the eggs, stirring frequently, until they're softly scrambled. Season with salt and pepper.
4. Sprinkle the shredded cheese and crumbled sausage over the cooked eggs, then remove the skillet from the heat.
5. Warm the low-carb tortillas in the microwave or a dry skillet until they're pliable.
6. Divide the egg mixture between the two tortillas, then roll each one tightly, tucking in the ends to create a burrito.
7. Serve the burritos warm with a side of salsa.

Nutritional Facts (per serving): Calories: 350; Protein: 20g; Fat: 25g; Carbohydrates: 10g (net); Fiber: 2g.

Tips: Make sure to cook the eggs gently to keep them soft and creamy. You could also add other vegetables like spinach or tomatoes for extra nutrients.

8. Sausage, Egg, and Cheese Bake

Preparation Time	Cooking Time	Serving Size
15 minutes	25 minutes	Serves 2

INGREDIENTS:

- » 4 large eggs
- » 2 breakfast sausage links, casing removed
- » 1/4 cup shredded cheddar cheese
- » 1/4 cup diced bell pepper
- » 1/4 cup diced onion
- » Salt and pepper to taste
- » 1 tablespoon olive oil

INSTRUCTIONS:

1. Preheat your oven to 375°F (190°C). Grease a small baking dish with a bit of the olive oil.
2. Heat the remaining olive oil in a skillet over medium heat. Add the sausage, breaking it up with a spoon, and cook until it's browned and cooked through.
3. Add the bell pepper and onion to the skillet, cooking until they're softened.
4. Spread the cooked sausage and vegetables in the prepared baking dish.
5. In a bowl, whisk the eggs with a bit of salt and pepper, then pour them over the sausage and vegetables.
6. Sprinkle the shredded cheese over the top of the egg mixture.
7. Bake in the preheated oven for about 20-25 minutes, until the eggs are set and the cheese is bubbly and golden.
8. Allow the bake to cool for a few minutes before slicing and serving.

Nutritional Facts (per serving): Calories: 370; Protein: 22g; Fat: 28g; Carbohydrates: 5g (net); Fiber: 1g.

Tips: For a spicier twist, consider using spicy sausage or adding a sprinkle of crushed red pepper flakes. Serve this bake with a side of fresh avocado or a drizzle of hot sauce for extra flavor.

9. Powerhouse Protein Smoothie

Preparation Time	Cooking Time	Serving Size
5 minutes	No cook time	Serves 2 (1 cup per person)

INGREDIENTS:

- » 1 cup unsweetened almond milk
- » 1/2 cup Greek yogurt
- » 1 scoop vanilla protein powder
- » 1/2 banana
- » 1 tablespoon almond butter
- » 1 cup fresh spinach
- » A handful of ice cubes

INSTRUCTIONS:

1. Combine all of the ingredients in a blender.
2. Blend until smooth and creamy.
3. Pour into two glasses and serve immediately.

Nutritional Facts (per serving): Calories: 200; Protein: 20g; Fat: 8g; Carbohydrates: 12g (net); Fiber: 2g.

Tips: Make sure to blend the smoothie well so that the spinach is completely incorporated. Feel free to add other protein-rich ingredients like chia seeds or flaxseeds.

10. Cauliflower Hash Browns

Preparation Time	Cooking Time	Serving Size
10 minutes	15 minutes	Serves 2 (2 hash browns per person)

INGREDIENTS:

- » 2 cups riced cauliflower
- » 1 large egg
- » 1/4 cup finely chopped onion
- » 1/4 cup shredded cheddar cheese
- » Salt and pepper to taste
- » 2 tablespoons olive oil

INSTRUCTIONS:

1. In a bowl, combine the riced cauliflower, egg, onion, and cheese. Season with salt and pepper.
2. Heat the olive oil in a non-stick skillet over medium heat.
3. Scoop a quarter of the cauliflower mixture onto the skillet and flatten it with a spatula to form a patty. Repeat with the rest of the mixture to form four patties.
4. Cook the patties until they're golden brown and crispy, about 5-7 minutes per side.
5. Serve the hash browns warm.

Nutritional Facts (per serving): Calories: 220; Protein: 10g; Fat: 16g; Carbohydrates: 10g (net); Fiber: 4g.

Tips: It's essential to get the cauliflower as dry as possible before making the hash browns to ensure they hold together well. Squeeze out any excess moisture with a cheesecloth or a clean kitchen towel.

Breakfast High Carb

11. Banana and Blueberry Pancakes

Preparation Time	Cooking Time	Serving Size
10 minutes	15 minutes	Serves 2 (2 pancakes per person)

INGREDIENTS:

- » 1 ripe banana
- » 2 large eggs
- » 1/2 cup blueberries
- » 1/2 teaspoon baking powder
- » 1 teaspoon vanilla extract
- » 2 tablespoons unsalted butter for frying
- » Sugar-free maple syrup, for serving

INSTRUCTIONS:

1. In a bowl, mash the ripe banana until there are no large chunks left.
2. Add the eggs, baking powder, and vanilla extract to the bowl and mix until well combined.
3. Gently fold the blueberries into the batter.
4. Heat a tablespoon of butter in a non-stick skillet over medium heat.
5. Spoon a quarter of the batter into the skillet for each pancake. Cook until you see bubbles form on the surface, about 2-3 minutes. Then flip and cook on the other side until golden brown, another 2-3 minutes.
6. Repeat with the remaining batter.
7. Serve the pancakes warm with a drizzle of sugar-free maple syrup.

Nutritional Facts (per serving): Calories: 240; Protein: 10g; Fat: 14g; Carbohydrates: 20g (net); Fiber: 3g.

Tips: Make sure to keep the heat at medium so the pancakes cook evenly without burning. These pancakes are naturally sweet from the banana, but feel free to add a bit of a sweetener like stevia if you prefer.

12. Oats and Apple Porridge

Preparation Time	Cooking Time	Serving Size
5 minutes	15 minutes	Serves 2

INGREDIENTS:

- » 1 cup rolled oats
- » 2 cups water or unsweetened almond milk
- » 1 apple, peeled and diced
- » 1 tablespoon honey or a sweetener of choice
- » 1/2 teaspoon cinnamon
- » A pinch of salt
- » Nuts or seeds for topping, optional

INSTRUCTIONS:

1. In a pot, bring the water or almond milk to a boil.
2. Stir in the oats and a pinch of salt, then reduce the heat to low.
3. Add the diced apple, honey, and cinnamon to the pot.
4. Simmer the porridge, stirring occasionally, until the oats are tender and the porridge is creamy, about 10-15 minutes.
5. Serve the porridge warm, topped with nuts or seeds if desired.

Nutritional Facts (per serving): Calories: 210; Protein: 6g; Fat: 3g; Carbohydrates: 40g (net); Fiber: 6g.

Tips: For creamier porridge, you can replace half the water with milk. Feel free to add other toppings like dried fruit, yogurt, or a drizzle of honey for extra flavor.

13. Whole Grain French Toast

Preparation Time	Cooking Time	Serving Size
10 minutes	10 minutes	Serves 2 (2 slices per person)

INGREDIENTS:

» 4 slices of whole grain bread
» 2 large eggs
» 1/2 cup low-fat milk
» 1 teaspoon vanilla extract
» 1/2 teaspoon cinnamon
» 2 teaspoons unsalted butter
» Fresh berries and sugar-free syrup, for serving

INSTRUCTIONS:

1. In a shallow dish, whisk together the eggs, milk, vanilla extract, and cinnamon.
2. Heat a teaspoon of butter in a non-stick skillet over medium heat.
3. Dip each slice of bread into the egg mixture, making sure to coat both sides well.
4. Cook the soaked bread slices in the skillet until golden brown on each side, about 2-3 minutes per side.
5. Repeat with the remaining bread slices and butter.
6. Serve the French toast warm with fresh berries and a drizzle of sugar-free syrup.

Nutritional Facts (per serving): Calories: 300; Protein: 15g; Fat: 10g; Carbohydrates: 40g (net); Fiber: 6g.

Tips: To ensure your French toast is soft and custardy on the inside but crisp on the outside, don't over-soak the bread. A quick dip in the egg mixture is enough!

14. Protein-Packed Quinoa Breakfast Bowl

Preparation Time	Cooking Time	Serving Size
5 minutes	15 minutes	Serves 2

INGREDIENTS:

» 1/2 cup quinoa
» 1 cup water
» A pinch of salt
» 1/2 cup low-fat Greek yogurt
» 1 banana, sliced
» 1 tablespoon chia seeds
» 1 tablespoon honey or a sweetener of choice
» Fresh berries, for topping

INSTRUCTIONS:

1. Rinse the quinoa under cold water to remove any bitter coating.
2. In a pot, bring the water to a boil. Add the rinsed quinoa and a pinch of salt, then reduce the heat to low.
3. Cover the pot and simmer until the quinoa is tender and the water has been absorbed, about 15 minutes.
4. Divide the cooked quinoa between two bowls.
5. Top each bowl with half of the Greek yogurt, banana slices, chia seeds, and a drizzle of honey.
6. Garnish with fresh berries before serving.

Nutritional Facts (per serving): Calories: 350; Protein: 15g; Fat: 5g; Carbohydrates: 60g (net); Fiber: 8g.

Tips: You can prepare the quinoa ahead of time and store it in the fridge for a quick and easy breakfast. Feel free to add other toppings like nuts, seeds, or dried fruit for extra nutrients and flavor.

15. Cinnamon Swirl Bagels

Preparation Time	**Cooking Time**	**Serving Size**
2 hours (includes rising time)	25 minutes	Makes 4 bagels

INGREDIENTS:

- » 2 cups bread flour
- » 1 teaspoon active dry yeast
- » 2 tablespoons white sugar
- » 3/4 cup warm water (about 110°F)
- » 1 teaspoon salt
- » 1 tablespoon ground cinnamon
- » 2 tablespoons brown sugar
- » 1 egg white, beaten for glazing

INSTRUCTIONS:

1. In a large bowl, combine the bread flour, yeast, and white sugar. Gradually add the warm water, stirring until a dough starts to form.
2. Transfer the dough onto a floured surface and knead for about 10 minutes, or until it is smooth and elastic.
3. Roll out the dough into a rectangle. Sprinkle the brown sugar and cinnamon evenly over the surface.
4. Roll the dough up tightly along the longer edge to create a log.
5. Divide the dough log into 4 equal pieces. Shape each piece into a bagel by pushing your thumb through the center and gently stretching the dough into a bagel shape.
6. Place the shaped bagels on a greased baking sheet, cover with a damp cloth, and let them rise for about 1 hour, or until they have doubled in size.
7. Preheat the oven to 375°F (190°C).
8. Brush the risen bagels with the beaten egg white.
9. Bake in the preheated oven for 20-25 minutes, or until the bagels are golden brown.

Nutritional Facts (per bagel): Calories: 260; Protein: 9g; Fat: 1g; Carbohydrates: 55g (net); Fiber: 2g.

Tips: You can use an egg wash to give your bagels a shiny, golden exterior. Be sure to let your bagels cool for a few minutes before slicing.

16. Maple-Sweetened Granola

Preparation Time	**Cooking Time**	**Serving Size**
10 minutes	20 minutes	Makes about 2 cups

INGREDIENTS:

- » 2 cups old-fashioned oats
- » 1/2 cup chopped nuts (such as almonds, walnuts, or pecans)
- » 1/4 cup seeds (like pumpkin or sunflower seeds)
- » 1/4 cup pure maple syrup
- » 2 tablespoons coconut oil, melted
- » 1/4 teaspoon salt
- » 1/2 teaspoon cinnamon
- » 1/2 cup dried fruit (optional)

INSTRUCTIONS:

1. Preheat the oven to 350°F (175°C) and line a baking sheet with parchment paper.
2. In a large bowl, combine the oats, nuts, and seeds.
3. In a small bowl, whisk together the maple syrup, melted coconut oil, salt, and cinnamon. Pour this mixture over the oats and stir until everything is well coated.
4. Spread the oat mixture out evenly on the prepared baking sheet.
5. Bake in the preheated oven for about 20 minutes, or until the granola is golden brown, stirring halfway through to ensure even baking.
6. If using, stir in the dried fruit after the granola has cooled.

Nutritional Facts (per 1/2 cup serving): Calories: 220; Protein: 6g; Fat: 12g; Carbohydrates: 25g (net); Fiber: 4g.

Tips: Store your granola in an airtight container at room temperature to keep it crunchy. You can also change up the nuts, seeds, and dried fruit to suit your taste preferences.

17. Berry Bliss Smoothie Bowl

Preparation Time	Cooking Time	Serving Size
10 minutes	0 minutes	Serves 2

INGREDIENTS:

» 2 cups mixed berries (fresh or frozen)
» 1 ripe banana
» 1/2 cup unsweetened almond milk
» 1 tablespoon chia seeds
» Toppings: sliced almonds, granola, fresh berries, shredded coconut

INSTRUCTIONS:

1. In a blender, combine the mixed berries, banana, almond milk, and chia seeds.
2. Blend until smooth, adding a bit more almond milk if needed to reach your desired consistency.
3. Divide the smoothie between two bowls.
4. Arrange your chosen toppings over the smoothie in each bowl. Serve immediately.

Nutritional Facts (per serving): Calories: 200; Protein: 4g; Fat: 3g; Carbohydrates: 40g (net); Fiber: 10g.

Tips: You can make your smoothie bowl more protein-packed by adding a scoop of your favorite protein powder. For a thicker smoothie bowl, use frozen fruit and less liquid.

18. Veggie-Packed Breakfast Burritos

Preparation Time	Cooking Time	Serving Size
10 minutes	20 minutes	Makes 2 burritos

INGREDIENTS:

» 2 large eggs
» Salt and pepper, to taste
» 1 tablespoon olive oil
» 1/2 bell pepper, chopped
» 1/2 onion, chopped
» 1/2 cup cooked black beans
» 1/2 cup shredded cheese
» 2 large whole grain tortillas
» Salsa and avocado slices, for serving

INSTRUCTIONS:

1. In a bowl, whisk the eggs with a pinch of salt and pepper.
2. Heat the olive oil in a non-stick skillet over medium heat.
3. Add the bell pepper and onion to the skillet. Cook until the vegetables are tender and the onion is translucent, about 5 minutes.
4. Pour the beaten eggs over the cooked vegetables in the skillet. Stir gently until the eggs are fully cooked.
5. Sprinkle the black beans and cheese over the egg mixture, then remove the skillet from heat.
6. Divide the egg and vegetable mixture between the two tortillas. Roll up each tortilla to form a burrito.
7. Serve the breakfast burritos warm, with salsa and avocado slices on the side.

Nutritional Facts (per burrito): Calories: 410; Protein: 20g; Fat: 18g; Carbohydrates: 45g (net); Fiber: 8g.

Tips: For an even more filling breakfast, add cooked, crumbled sausage or bacon to your burritos. You can also make these burritos ahead of time and reheat them in the microwave for a quick and easy breakfast.

19. Sweet Potato and Black Bean Breakfast Hash

Preparation Time	Cooking Time	Serving Size
10 minutes	30 minutes	Serves 2

INGREDIENTS:

- » 1 large sweet potato, peeled and diced
- » 1 tablespoon olive oil
- » 1/2 onion, diced
- » 1 bell pepper, diced
- » 1/2 cup cooked black beans
- » Salt and pepper, to taste
- » 2 large eggs
- » Fresh cilantro, for garnish

INSTRUCTIONS:

1. Heat the olive oil in a large skillet over medium heat. Add the sweet potato and cook until it starts to soften, about 10 minutes.
2. Add the diced onion and bell pepper to the skillet. Continue cooking until the vegetables are tender and the sweet potato is cooked through, about 10 more minutes.
3. Stir in the black beans and season with salt and pepper to taste.
4. Make two wells in the vegetable hash and crack an egg into each well.
5. Cover the skillet and cook until the eggs are done to your liking.
6. Garnish with fresh cilantro before serving.

Nutritional Facts (per serving): Calories: 370; Protein: 12g; Fat: 12g; Carbohydrates: 55g (net); Fiber: 10g.

Tips: For a spicier kick, consider adding some chili powder or smoked paprika to your breakfast hash. This dish can easily be customized with your favorite vegetables or spices.

20. Pumpkin Spice Oatmeal

Preparation Time	Cooking Time	Serving Size
5 minutes	10 minutes	Serves 2

INGREDIENTS:

- » 1 cup old-fashioned oats
- » 2 cups water or milk
- » 1/2 cup pumpkin puree
- » 1 teaspoon pumpkin pie spice
- » 1-2 tablespoons maple syrup or sweetener of choice
- » Toppings: chopped nuts, dried fruit, a dollop of Greek yogurt

INSTRUCTIONS:

1. In a pot, bring the water or milk to a boil. Add the oats and reduce heat to a simmer.
2. Cook the oats, stirring occasionally, until they are soft and the liquid is mostly absorbed, about 5 minutes.
3. Stir in the pumpkin puree, pumpkin pie spice, and sweetener. Cook for another 2-3 minutes, until heated through.
4. Divide the oatmeal between two bowls.
5. Top with your favorite toppings before serving.

Nutritional Facts (per serving): Calories: 270; Protein: 7g; Fat: 4g; Carbohydrates: 52g (net); Fiber: 8g.

Tips: To make this oatmeal even creamier, try cooking the oats in milk instead of water. For added texture, top with chopped nuts or dried fruit.

21. Crunchy Chicken Salad Wraps

Preparation Time	Cooking Time	Serving Size
20 minutes	0 minutes	Serves 2

INGREDIENTS:

» 1 cup cooked chicken, shredded
» 1/4 cup mayonnaise
» 1 stalk celery, diced
» 1 green onion, finely chopped
» Salt and pepper, to taste
» 4 large lettuce leaves (like romaine or iceberg)
» 1/4 cup sliced almonds

INSTRUCTIONS:

1. In a medium bowl, mix together the shredded chicken, mayonnaise, diced celery, and chopped green onion.
2. Season the chicken salad with salt and pepper to taste.
3. Lay out the lettuce leaves on a flat surface. Divide the chicken salad evenly among the lettuce leaves.
4. Sprinkle the sliced almonds over the top of the chicken salad.
5. Roll up each lettuce leaf to form a wrap. Serve immediately.

Nutritional Facts (per serving): Calories: 350; Protein: 25g; Fat: 24g; Carbohydrates: 5g (net); Fiber: 3g.

Tips: For added flavor, you might consider adding a squeeze of lemon juice or some fresh herbs to your chicken salad. You can also substitute the mayonnaise with Greek yogurt for a lighter option.

22. Greek Style Cauliflower Rice Bowl

Preparation Time	Cooking Time	Serving Size
15 minutes	10 minutes	Serves 2

INGREDIENTS:

» 2 cups riced cauliflower
» 1 tablespoon olive oil
» 1/2 cup cherry tomatoes, halved
» 1/2 cup cucumber, diced
» 1/4 cup Kalamata olives, sliced
» 1/4 cup feta cheese, crumbled
» 2 tablespoons fresh lemon juice
» Salt and pepper, to taste
» Fresh parsley, for garnish

INSTRUCTIONS:

1. Heat the olive oil in a skillet over medium heat. Add the riced cauliflower and cook until it is tender, about 5-7 minutes.
2. In a large bowl, combine the cooked cauliflower rice, cherry tomatoes, cucumber, and Kalamata olives.
3. Drizzle the salad with fresh lemon juice, then season with salt and pepper to taste.
4. Divide the salad between two bowls. Top each bowl with crumbled feta cheese.
5. Garnish with fresh parsley before serving.

Nutritional Facts (per serving): Calories: 200; Protein: 7g; Fat: 14g; Carbohydrates: 12g (net); Fiber: 4g.

Tips: If you'd like to add some protein to this bowl, consider topping it with some grilled chicken or shrimp. You can also add additional Greek flavors by including some tzatziki sauce or hummus.

23. Zucchini Noodle Pasta with Pesto

Preparation Time	Cooking Time	Serving Size
20 minutes	5 minutes	Serves 2

INGREDIENTS:

» 2 large zucchinis
» 1/2 cup basil pesto (homemade or store-bought)
» Salt and pepper, to taste
» 2 tablespoons grated Parmesan cheese
» Fresh basil leaves, for garnish

INSTRUCTIONS:

1. Using a spiralizer or a vegetable peeler, turn the zucchinis into noodles.
2. In a large skillet over medium heat, add the zucchini noodles and cook for 2-3 minutes, just until they are tender but not too soft.
3. Remove the skillet from the heat. Add the pesto to the zucchini noodles and toss well to combine.
4. Season the zucchini noodle pasta with salt and pepper to taste.
5. Divide the pasta between two bowls. Sprinkle each serving with grated Parmesan cheese.
6. Garnish with fresh basil leaves before serving.

Nutritional Facts (per serving): Calories: 210; Protein: 6g; Fat: 18g; Carbohydrates: 8g (net); Fiber: 3g.

Tips: You can add more protein to this dish by topping it with grilled chicken or shrimp. Feel free to add other veggies like cherry tomatoes or bell peppers for added color and flavor.

24. Rainbow Vegetable Skewers

Preparation Time	Cooking Time	Serving Size
15 minutes	10 minutes	Makes 4 skewers

INGREDIENTS:

» 1 bell pepper, cut into chunks (choose different colors for a rainbow effect)
» 1 zucchini, sliced into thick rounds
» 1 red onion, cut into chunks
» 8 cherry tomatoes
» 8 button mushrooms
» 2 tablespoons olive oil
» Salt and pepper, to taste

INSTRUCTIONS:

1. Preheat your grill to medium-high heat.
2. Thread the vegetables onto skewers, alternating the types of vegetables to create a rainbow effect.
3. Brush the skewered vegetables with olive oil, then season with salt and pepper.
4. Grill the skewers for about 10 minutes, turning occasionally, until the vegetables are tender and lightly charred.
5. Serve the vegetable skewers hot off the grill.

Nutritional Facts (per skewer): Calories: 110; Protein: 2g; Fat: 7g; Carbohydrates: 10g (net); Fiber: 3g.

Tips: Feel free to use any vegetables you like for these skewers. Other great options include eggplant, yellow squash, or sweet potatoes. If you're using wooden skewers, be sure to soak them in water for at least 30 minutes before grilling to prevent them from burning.

25. Spicy Shrimp and Avocado Lettuce Wraps

Preparation Time	Cooking Time	Serving Size
15 minutes	10 minutes	Serves 2

INGREDIENTS:

» 12 large shrimps, peeled and deveined
» 1 tablespoon olive oil
» 1 teaspoon chili powder
» Salt and pepper, to taste
» 1 avocado, sliced
» 4 large lettuce leaves (like romaine or iceberg)
» Fresh cilantro, for garnish
» Lime wedges, for serving

INSTRUCTIONS:

1. Toss the shrimps with olive oil, chili powder, salt, and pepper.
2. Heat a skillet over medium-high heat. Add the shrimps and cook until they turn pink, about 2-3 minutes per side.
3. Lay out the lettuce leaves on a flat surface. Divide the cooked shrimps and avocado slices evenly among the lettuce leaves.
4. Garnish each lettuce wrap with fresh cilantro.
5. Serve the wraps with lime wedges on the side.

Nutritional Facts (per serving): Calories: 290; Protein: 18g; Fat: 21g; Carbohydrates: 9g (net); Fiber: 6g.

Tips: Remember not to overcook the shrimps, as they can become tough. A hint of lime juice can brighten the flavors beautifully.

26. Mediterranean Tuna Salad

Preparation Time	Cooking Time	Serving Size
15 minutes	0 minutes	Serves 2

INGREDIENTS:

» 1 can (5 ounces) tuna, drained
» 1/4 cup Kalamata olives, sliced
» 1/4 cup cherry tomatoes, halved
» 1/4 cup cucumber, diced
» 1/4 cup red onion, finely chopped
» 2 tablespoons olive oil
» 1 tablespoon fresh lemon juice
» Salt and pepper, to taste
» Fresh parsley, for garnish

INSTRUCTIONS:

1. In a bowl, mix together the tuna, olives, cherry tomatoes, cucumber, and red onion.
2. In a separate small bowl, whisk together the olive oil and lemon juice. Season with salt and pepper to taste.
3. Pour the dressing over the tuna mixture and toss well to combine.
4. Divide the salad between two plates. Garnish with fresh parsley before serving.

Nutritional Facts (per serving): Calories: 210; Protein: 20g; Fat: 12g; Carbohydrates: 6g (net); Fiber: 1g.

Tips: Try to choose a high-quality, sustainably caught canned tuna for the best flavor. You can add more Mediterranean ingredients like feta cheese or artichoke hearts for a more substantial salad.

27. Egg Roll in a Bowl

Preparation Time	Cooking Time	Serving Size
10 minutes	15 minutes	Serves 2

INGREDIENTS:

» 1/2-pound ground pork
» 2 cups shredded cabbage
» 1 carrot, shredded
» 2 green onions, sliced
» 2 cloves garlic, minced
» 1 tablespoon soy sauce
» 1 teaspoon sesame oil
» Salt and pepper, to taste

INSTRUCTIONS:

1. In a large skillet over medium-high heat, cook the ground pork until no longer pink, breaking it up into crumbles.
2. Add the shredded cabbage, shredded carrot, green onions, and minced garlic to the skillet. Cook until the vegetables are tender, about 5-7 minutes.
3. Stir in the soy sauce and sesame oil, then season with salt and pepper to taste.
4. Serve the "egg roll" mixture hot, right out of the skillet.

Nutritional Facts (per serving): Calories: 380; Protein: 20g; Fat: 28g; Carbohydrates: 10g (net); Fiber: 3g.

Tips: Feel free to add other typical egg roll ingredients, such as bean sprouts or mushrooms, to this dish. A drizzle of sriracha sauce can spice things up.

28. Grilled Chicken Cobb Salad

Preparation Time	Cooking Time	Serving Size
15 minutes	15 minutes	Serves 2

INGREDIENTS:

» 2 boneless, skinless chicken breasts
» Salt and pepper, to taste
» 4 cups chopped romaine lettuce
» 2 hard-boiled eggs, sliced
» 1 avocado, diced
» 1/4 cup crumbled blue cheese
» 2 slices cooked bacon, crumbled
» Your favorite low-carb salad dressing

INSTRUCTIONS:

1. Preheat your grill to medium-high heat. Season the chicken breasts with salt and pepper.
2. Grill the chicken until it is cooked through and no longer pink in the center, about 6-7 minutes per side. Let the chicken rest for a few minutes, then slice it.
3. Divide the chopped romaine lettuce between two plates. Top each salad with sliced chicken, hard-boiled eggs, diced avocado, crumbled blue cheese, and crumbled bacon.
4. Drizzle each salad with your favorite low-carb dressing before serving.

Nutritional Facts (per serving): Calories: 510; Protein: 40g; Fat: 33g; Carbohydrates: 10g (net); Fiber: 7g.

Tips: Grill the chicken ahead of time for a quick and easy meal prep. You can also substitute the blue cheese with feta or goat cheese for a different flavor profile.

29. Crispy Baked Tofu Stir Fry

Preparation Time	Cooking Time	Serving Size
15 minutes	30 minutes	Serves 2

INGREDIENTS:

» 1 block (14 ounces) firm tofu, drained and cubed
» 2 tablespoons olive oil, divided
» Salt and pepper, to taste
» 2 cups mixed vegetables (such as bell peppers, broccoli, and carrots)
» 2 tablespoons soy sauce
» 1 teaspoon sesame seeds, for garnish

INSTRUCTIONS:

1. Preheat your oven to 400°F. Toss the tofu cubes with 1 tablespoon of olive oil, salt, and pepper. Spread the tofu cubes in a single layer on a baking sheet.
2. Bake the tofu for 25-30 minutes, or until it is crispy and golden brown.
3. Meanwhile, heat the remaining 1 tablespoon of olive oil in a skillet over medium heat. Add the mixed vegetables and cook until they are tender, about 5-7 minutes.
4. Stir in the soy sauce and cooked tofu. Toss everything together until the tofu and vegetables are well coated in the sauce.
5. Serve the stir fry hot, garnished with sesame seeds.

Nutritional Facts (per serving): Calories: 350; Protein: 18g; Fat: 20g; Carbohydrates: 24g (net); Fiber: 6g.

Tips: Remember to press the tofu before baking to remove excess moisture. This will help the tofu become crispy in the oven. You can use any mix of vegetables you like for this stir fry.

30. Cheesy Spinach Stuffed Chicken Breast

Preparation Time	Cooking Time	Serving Size
20 minutes	25 minutes	Serves 2

INGREDIENTS:

» 2 boneless, skinless chicken breasts
» Salt and pepper, to taste
» 1 cup fresh spinach, chopped
» 1/2 cup cream cheese
» 1/4 cup grated Parmesan cheese
» 1 tablespoon olive oil

INSTRUCTIONS:

1. Preheat your oven to 375°F. Season the chicken breasts with salt and pepper.
2. Using a sharp knife, cut a pocket into the side of each chicken breast. Be careful not to cut all the way through.
3. In a bowl, mix together the chopped spinach, cream cheese, and grated Parmesan. Stuff this mixture into the pockets you cut in the chicken breasts.
4. Heat the olive oil in an oven-safe skillet over medium-high heat. Add the stuffed chicken breasts and cook until they are golden brown on each side, about 3-4 minutes per side.
5. Transfer the skillet to the oven and bake the chicken for 15-20 minutes, or until the chicken is cooked through and no longer pink in the center.
6. Serve the chicken hot, drizzled with any juices left in the skillet.

Nutritional Facts (per serving): Calories: 460; Protein: 40g; Fat: 30g; Carbohydrates: 3g (net); Fiber: 1g.

Tips: Feel free to add other ingredients to the stuffing, like sun-dried tomatoes or feta cheese. You can also wrap the chicken breasts in bacon for added flavor and crispiness.

Lunch High Carb

31. Lentil and Sweet Potato Salad

Preparation Time	Cooking Time	Serving Size
15 minutes	20 minutes	Serves 2

INGREDIENTS:

» 1 cup green lentils, rinsed
» 2 cups sweet potatoes, peeled and diced
» 1 red bell pepper, diced
» 1/2 red onion, finely chopped
» 2 tablespoons fresh parsley, chopped
» 2 tablespoons fresh mint, chopped
» 2 tablespoons lemon juice
» 2 tablespoons olive oil
» Salt and pepper, to taste

INSTRUCTIONS:

1. In a medium saucepan, bring 3 cups of water to a boil. Add the rinsed lentils and cook until they are tender but still hold their shape, about 15-20 minutes. Drain and set aside.
2. In a separate pot, steam or boil the sweet potatoes until they are just fork-tender, about 10 minutes. Drain and set aside.
3. In a large bowl, combine the cooked lentils, sweet potatoes, red bell pepper, red onion, parsley, and mint.
4. In a small bowl, whisk together the lemon juice, olive oil, salt, and pepper. Pour the dressing over the salad ingredients and toss gently to coat.
5. Adjust the seasoning if necessary. Serve the lentil and sweet potato salad at room temperature or chilled.

Nutritional Facts (per serving): Calories: 300; Protein: 14g; Fat: 6g; Carbohydrates: 50g (net); Fiber: 12g.

Tips: To add more flavor and texture, you can include crumbled feta cheese or chopped toasted nuts, such as walnuts or almonds, to this salad. It can be enjoyed as a side dish or a light vegetarian main course.

32. Chickpea Avocado Toast

Preparation Time	Cooking Time	Serving Size
10 minutes	0 minutes	Serves 2

INGREDIENTS:

» 4 slices whole grain bread
» 1 ripe avocado
» 1 can (15 ounces) chickpeas, drained and rinsed
» 1 tablespoon lemon juice
» 1 tablespoon olive oil
» 1 clove garlic, minced
» 1/4 teaspoon cumin
» Salt and pepper, to taste
» Fresh cilantro, for garnish

INSTRUCTIONS:

1. Toast the slices of whole grain bread until they are golden and crisp.
2. In a bowl, mash the ripe avocado with a fork until it reaches your desired consistency. Season with salt and pepper to taste.
3. In a separate bowl, combine the drained and rinsed chickpeas, lemon juice, olive oil, minced garlic, cumin, salt, and pepper. Mash the chickpeas slightly with a fork or potato masher to create a chunky mixture.
4. Spread the mashed avocado evenly onto each slice of toasted bread.
5. Top the avocado with the mashed chickpea mixture, dividing it equally among the slices of bread.
6. Garnish the chickpea avocado toast with fresh cilantro.

Nutritional Facts (per serving): Calories: 400; Protein: 16g; Fat: 16g; Carbohydrates: 50g (net); Fiber: 16g.

Tips: Feel free to customize your chickpea avocado toast with additional toppings, such as sliced cherry tomatoes, crumbled feta cheese, or a drizzle of hot sauce. It makes for a satisfying and nutritious breakfast or snack option.

33. Butternut Squash and Quinoa Stew

Preparation Time	Cooking Time	Serving Size
15 minutes	35 minutes	Serves 2

INGREDIENTS:

» 1 tablespoon olive oil
» 1 medium onion, chopped
» 2 cloves garlic, minced
» 3 cups butternut squash, peeled and diced
» 1 cup quinoa, rinsed
» 4 cups vegetable broth
» 1 teaspoon dried thyme
» 1/2 teaspoon ground cumin
» Salt and pepper, to taste
» Fresh parsley or cilantro, for garnish

INSTRUCTIONS:

1. In a large pot, heat the olive oil over medium heat. Add the chopped onion and minced garlic, and sauté until they are fragrant and lightly golden.
2. Add the diced butternut squash and cook for another 5 minutes, stirring occasionally.
3. Stir in the rinsed quinoa, vegetable broth, dried thyme, ground cumin, salt, and pepper. Bring the mixture to a boil.
4. Reduce the heat to low, cover the pot, and let the stew simmer for about 20-25 minutes, or until the quinoa and butternut squash are tender.
5. Adjust the seasoning if necessary. Serve the butternut squash and quinoa stew hot, garnished with fresh parsley or cilantro.

Nutritional Facts (per serving): Calories: 300; Protein: 9g; Fat: 6g; Carbohydrates: 55g (net); Fiber: 8g.

Tips: Feel free to add other vegetables like spinach or kale to the stew for added nutrients. For extra richness, stir in a tablespoon of coconut milk or cream.

34. Mediterranean Couscous Salad

Preparation Time	Cooking Time	Serving Size
15 minutes	10 minutes	Serves 2

INGREDIENTS:

» 1 cup couscous
» 1 1/4 cups vegetable broth
» 1/2 English cucumber, diced
» 1 cup cherry tomatoes, halved
» 1/2 red onion, finely chopped
» 1/2 cup Kalamata olives, sliced
» 1/4 cup crumbled feta cheese
» 2 tablespoons extra virgin olive oil
» 2 tablespoons lemon juice
» 1 teaspoon dried oregano
» Salt and pepper, to taste
» Fresh parsley, for garnish

INSTRUCTIONS:

1. In a saucepan, bring the vegetable broth to a boil. Remove the pan from the heat, add the couscous, cover, and let it sit for 5 minutes.
2. Fluff the couscous with a fork and transfer it to a large bowl.
3. Add the diced cucumber, halved cherry tomatoes, finely chopped red onion, sliced Kalamata olives, and crumbled feta cheese to the bowl.
4. In a separate small bowl, whisk together the extra virgin olive oil, lemon juice, dried oregano, salt, and pepper.
5. Pour the dressing over the couscous salad and toss gently to combine.
6. Adjust the seasoning if needed. Garnish the Mediterranean couscous salad with fresh parsley before serving.

Nutritional Facts (per serving): Calories: 280; Protein: 8g; Fat: 10g; Carbohydrates: 40g (net); Fiber: 6g.

Tips: You can add additional Mediterranean ingredients like roasted red peppers or artichoke hearts for more flavor and variety. This salad can be served as a refreshing side dish or a light main course.

35. Veggie-Packed Burrito Bowl

Preparation Time	Cooking Time	Serving Size
15 minutes	15 minutes	Serves 2

INGREDIENTS:

» For the Burrito Bowl:
» 2 cups cooked brown rice
» 1 can (15 ounces) black beans, drained and rinsed
» 1 cup corn kernels (fresh or frozen)
» 1 red bell pepper, diced
» 1 cup cherry tomatoes, halved
» 1/2 red onion, finely chopped
» 1 avocado, sliced
» Fresh cilantro, for garnish
» Lime wedges, for serving
» For the Lime Cilantro Dressing:
» 1/4 cup fresh lime juice
» 2 tablespoons olive oil
» 1/4 cup chopped fresh cilantro
» 1 clove garlic, minced
» Salt and pepper, to taste

INSTRUCTIONS:

1. In a large bowl, combine the cooked brown rice, black beans, corn kernels, diced red bell pepper, halved cherry tomatoes, and finely chopped red onion.
2. In a separate small bowl, whisk together the fresh lime juice, olive oil, chopped cilantro, minced garlic, salt, and pepper to make the dressing.
3. Pour the dressing over the burrito bowl ingredients and toss gently to coat.
4. Divide the burrito bowl mixture into four serving bowls. Top each bowl with sliced avocado and garnish with fresh cilantro.
5. Serve the veggie-packed burrito bowls with lime wedges on the side.

Nutritional Facts (per serving): Calories: 350; Protein: 10g; Fat: 10g; Carbohydrates: 57g (net); Fiber: 12g.

Tips: Feel free to customize your burrito bowl with additional toppings like salsa, Greek yogurt, or shredded cheese. You can also add grilled chicken, shrimp, or tofu for extra protein.

36. Grilled Chicken Pasta Salad

Preparation Time	Cooking Time	Chilling Time
15 minutes	10 minutes	1 hour

Serving Size: Serves 4

INGREDIENTS:

- For the Salad:
- 8 ounces rotini pasta
- 2 grilled chicken breasts, sliced
- 1 cup cherry tomatoes, halved
- 1/2 English cucumber, diced
- 1/4 red onion, thinly sliced
- 1/4 cup black olives, sliced
- 1/4 cup crumbled feta cheese
- Fresh basil leaves, for garnish
- For the Dressing:
- 2 tablespoons extra virgin olive oil
- 1 tablespoon red wine vinegar
- 1 teaspoon Dijon mustard
- 1 clove garlic, minced
- Salt and pepper, to taste

INSTRUCTIONS:

1. Cook the rotini pasta according to the package instructions until al dente. Drain and rinse with cold water to cool it down.
2. In a large bowl, combine the cooked rotini pasta, sliced grilled chicken breasts, halved cherry tomatoes, diced cucumber, thinly sliced red onion, sliced black olives, and crumbled feta cheese.
3. In a separate small bowl, whisk together the extra virgin olive oil, red wine vinegar, Dijon mustard, minced garlic, salt, and pepper to make the dressing.
4. Pour the dressing over the pasta salad and toss gently to coat.
5. Cover the bowl and refrigerate the pasta salad for at least 1 hour to allow the flavors to meld together.
6. Garnish the grilled chicken pasta salad with fresh basil leaves before serving.

Nutritional Facts (per serving): Calories: 400; Protein: 25g; Fat: 14g; Carbohydrates: 45g (net); Fiber: 4g.

Tips: Feel free to add other ingredients like diced bell peppers, artichoke hearts, or sun-dried tomatoes to customize your pasta salad. It can be served as a main dish or a side dish for a picnic or barbecue.

37. Black Bean and Corn Quesadillas

Preparation Time	Cooking Time	Serving Size
10 minutes	15 minutes	Serves 4

INGREDIENTS:

» 8 small flour tortillas
» 1 can (15 ounces) black beans, drained and rinsed
» 1 cup corn kernels (fresh or frozen)
» 1/2 red bell pepper, diced
» 1/2 small red onion, finely chopped
» 1 jalapeño pepper, seeded and minced (optional)
» 1/2 cup shredded cheddar cheese
» 1/2 cup shredded Monterey Jack cheese
» Fresh cilantro, for garnish
» Sour cream, salsa, or guacamole, for serving

INSTRUCTIONS:

1. Preheat a large skillet or griddle over medium heat.
2. Place a tortilla on the skillet and sprinkle half of the tortilla with a layer of black beans, corn kernels, diced red bell pepper, finely chopped red onion, minced jalapeño pepper (if using), and a mixture of shredded cheddar and Monterey Jack cheese.
3. Fold the other half of the tortilla over the filling to create a half-moon shape.
4. Cook the quesadilla for about 2-3 minutes on each side until the tortilla is crispy and the cheese is melted. Repeat with the remaining tortillas and filling ingredients.
5. Transfer the cooked quesadillas to a cutting board and let them cool for a minute before cutting each into three wedges.
6. Garnish the black bean and corn quesadillas with fresh cilantro. Serve with sour cream, salsa, or guacamole on the side.

Nutritional Facts (per serving): Calories: 350; Protein: 14g; Fat: 12g; Carbohydrates: 47g (net); Fiber: 7g.

Tips: Feel free to customize your quesadillas by adding sliced avocado, diced tomatoes, or chopped fresh herbs like basil or cilantro. Serve them as a delicious and satisfying lunch or dinner option.

38. Asian-Inspired Noodle Bowl

Preparation Time	Cooking Time	Serving Size
15 minutes	15 minutes	Serves 4

INGREDIENTS:

» For the Noodle Bowl:
» 8 ounces rice noodles
» 1 tablespoon vegetable oil
» 1 cup broccoli florets
» 1 carrot, julienned
» 1 red bell pepper, thinly sliced
» 1 cup snow peas
» 1 cup sliced mushrooms
» 1/4 cup chopped green onions
» Sesame seeds, for garnish
» For the Sauce:
» 2 tablespoons soy sauce
» 2 tablespoons hoisin sauce
» 1 tablespoon rice vinegar
» 1 tablespoon honey or maple syrup
» 1 teaspoon sesame oil
» 1 clove garlic, minced
» 1/2 teaspoon grated ginger

INSTRUCTIONS:

1. Cook the rice noodles according to the package instructions until al dente. Drain and rinse with cold water to cool them down.
2. In a large skillet or wok, heat the vegetable oil over medium-high heat. Add the broccoli florets, julienned carrot, thinly sliced red bell pepper, snow peas, and sliced mushrooms. Stir-fry the vegetables for about 5-7 minutes, until they are crisp-tender.
3. In a small bowl, whisk together the soy sauce, hoisin sauce, rice vinegar, honey or maple syrup, sesame oil, minced garlic, and grated ginger to make the sauce.
4. Add the cooked rice noodles, chopped green onions, and the sauce to the skillet with the stir-fried vegetables. Toss everything together until well coated and heated through.
5. Garnish the Asian-inspired noodle bowl with sesame seeds before serving.

Nutritional Facts (per serving): Calories: 320; Protein: 6g; Fat: 4g; Carbohydrates: 65g (net); Fiber: 5g.

Tips: You can customize your noodle bowl by adding cooked chicken, shrimp, or tofu for extra protein. Feel free to add other vegetables like bean sprouts or bok choy for variation. Enjoy this flavorful and satisfying Asian-inspired dish!

39. Hearty Lentil Soup with Whole Grain Bread

Preparation Time	Cooking Time	Serving Size
15 minutes	45 minutes	Serves 2

INGREDIENTS:

» 1 tablespoon olive oil
» 1 small onion, chopped
» 2 cloves garlic, minced
» 1 carrot, diced
» 1 celery stalk, diced
» 1 cup dried green or brown lentils, rinsed
» 4 cups vegetable broth
» 1 bay leaf
» 1 teaspoon dried thyme
» Salt and pepper, to taste
» Fresh parsley, for garnish
» Whole grain bread, for serving

INSTRUCTIONS:

1. Heat the olive oil in a large pot over medium heat. Add the chopped onion and minced garlic, and sauté until they are fragrant and lightly golden.
2. Add the diced carrot and celery to the pot, and cook for a few more minutes until they begin to soften.
3. Add the rinsed lentils, vegetable broth, bay leaf, dried thyme, salt, and pepper to the pot. Stir well to combine.
4. Bring the soup to a boil, then reduce the heat to low and let it simmer, partially covered, for about 35-40 minutes or until the lentils are tender.
5. Remove the bay leaf and adjust the seasoning if necessary.
6. Ladle the hearty lentil soup into bowls, garnish with fresh parsley, and serve with slices of whole grain bread.

Nutritional Facts (per serving): Calories: 350; Protein: 18g; Fat: 6g; Carbohydrates: 60g (net); Fiber: 18g.

Tips: Feel free to add additional vegetables like diced potatoes or spinach to the soup. You can also squeeze fresh lemon juice over the soup before serving to add a touch of acidity.

40. Sweet Potato Black Bean Burgers

Preparation Time	Cooking Time	Serving Size
20 minutes	25 minutes	Serves 2

INGREDIENTS:

» 1 large sweet potato, cooked and mashed
» 1 can (15 ounces) black beans, drained and rinsed
» 1/4 cup finely chopped red onion
» 1/4 cup finely chopped bell pepper (any color)
» 1/4 cup breadcrumbs
» 1/4 cup cornmeal
» 1 teaspoon chili powder
» 1/2 teaspoon cumin
» Salt and pepper, to taste
» Olive oil, for cooking
» Burger buns and desired toppings, for serving

INSTRUCTIONS:

1. In a large bowl, combine the mashed sweet potato, drained black beans, finely chopped red onion, finely chopped bell pepper, breadcrumbs, cornmeal, chili powder, cumin, salt, and pepper. Mix well until all ingredients are evenly combined.
2. Divide the mixture into two portions, then shape each portion into a burger patty.
3. Heat a drizzle of olive oil in a skillet over medium heat. Place the burger patties in the skillet and cook for about 5-6 minutes on each side, or until they are golden brown and heated through.
4. Toast the burger buns if desired, then assemble the sweet potato black bean burgers with your favorite toppings.
5. Serve the burgers alongside a side salad or roasted vegetables.

Nutritional Facts (per serving): Calories: 400; Protein: 15g; Fat: 6g; Carbohydrates: 75g (net); Fiber: 15g.

Tips: Feel free to customize your burgers by adding additional spices or herbs, such as paprika or fresh cilantro. You can also serve them with a side of homemade sweet potato fries for a complete meal.

Dinner Low Carb

41. Garlic Butter Steak Bites

Preparation Time	Cooking Time	Serving Size
10 minutes	10 minutes	Serves 2

INGREDIENTS:

» 12 ounces sirloin steak, cut into bite-sized pieces
» 2 tablespoons butter
» 4 cloves garlic, minced
» Salt and pepper, to taste
» Fresh parsley, chopped, for garnish

INSTRUCTIONS:

1. Heat a large skillet over medium-high heat. Add the butter and let it melt.
2. Add the minced garlic to the skillet and sauté for about 30 seconds until fragrant.
3. Season the steak bites with salt and pepper, then add them to the skillet. Cook for about 2-3 minutes per side, or until they reach your desired level of doneness.
4. Remove the skillet from the heat and let the steak bites rest for a couple of minutes.
5. Transfer the steak bites to a serving plate and sprinkle them with fresh parsley.
6. Serve the garlic butter steak bites as an appetizer or as a main course with your favorite side dishes.

Nutritional Facts (per serving): Calories: 400; Protein: 30g; Fat: 28g; Carbohydrates: 2g (net); Fiber: 0g.

Tips: For an extra burst of flavor, you can squeeze fresh lemon juice over the steak bites before serving. Feel free to adjust the amount of garlic according to your preference.

42. Balsamic Chicken with Brussels Sprouts

Preparation Time	**Cooking Time**	**Serving Size**
15 minutes	25 minutes	Serves 2

INGREDIENTS:

» 2 boneless, skinless chicken breasts
» Salt and pepper, to taste
» 1 tablespoon olive oil
» 1 tablespoon balsamic vinegar
» 2 tablespoons honey
» 2 cloves garlic, minced
» 1 cup Brussels sprouts, halved
» Fresh parsley, chopped, for garnish

INSTRUCTIONS:

1. Preheat your oven to 400°F (200°C).
2. Season the chicken breasts with salt and pepper on both sides.
3. Heat the olive oil in an oven-safe skillet over medium-high heat. Add the chicken breasts and sear them for about 2-3 minutes per side until golden brown.
4. In a small bowl, whisk together the balsamic vinegar, honey, and minced garlic.
5. Pour the balsamic mixture over the chicken breasts in the skillet.
6. Add the halved Brussels sprouts to the skillet, arranging them around the chicken.
7. Transfer the skillet to the preheated oven and bake for about 18-20 minutes, or until the chicken is cooked through and the Brussels sprouts are tender.
8. Remove the skillet from the oven and let it rest for a couple of minutes.
9. Sprinkle the balsamic chicken and Brussels sprouts with fresh parsley before serving.

Nutritional Facts (per serving): Calories: 350; Protein: 30g; Fat: 10g; Carbohydrates: 30g (net); Fiber: 5g.

Tips: You can add other vegetables like cherry tomatoes or sliced bell peppers to the skillet for added color and flavor. Serve the balsamic chicken with Brussels sprouts alongside cooked quinoa or brown rice.

43. Crispy Skin Salmon with Zoodles

Preparation Time	Cooking Time	Serving Size
10 minutes	15 minutes	Serves 2

INGREDIENTS:

» 2 skin-on salmon fillets
» Salt and pepper, to taste
» 1 tablespoon olive oil
» 2 medium zucchini, spiralized into zoodles
» 2 cloves garlic, minced
» Juice of 1 lemon
» Fresh dill, chopped, for garnish

INSTRUCTIONS:

1. Pat the salmon fillets dry with paper towels, then season both sides with salt and pepper.
2. Heat the olive oil in a skillet over medium-high heat. Place the salmon fillets in the skillet, skin-side down.
3. Cook the salmon for about 4-5 minutes on the skin side until the skin is crispy and golden brown. Flip the fillets and cook for an additional 3-4 minutes, or until the salmon is cooked to your preferred doneness.
4. Remove the salmon from the skillet and set aside.
5. In the same skillet, add the minced garlic and cook for about 1 minute until fragrant.
6. Add the zoodles to the skillet and sauté them for about 2-3 minutes until they are tender-crisp.
7. Squeeze the lemon juice over the zoodles and season with salt and pepper to taste. Toss everything together.
8. Divide the zoodles between two plates and place a salmon fillet on top of each portion.
9. Garnish with fresh dill and serve the crispy skin salmon with zoodles immediately.

Nutritional Facts (per serving): Calories: 400; Protein: 40g; Fat: 22g; Carbohydrates: 10g (net); Fiber: 4g.

Tips: Feel free to add additional seasonings or spices to the salmon fillets, such as paprika or dried herbs. You can also top the dish with a dollop of Greek yogurt or sour cream for added creaminess.

44. Stuffed Bell Peppers with Ground Turkey

Preparation Time	Cooking Time	Serving Size
20 minutes	40 minutes	Serves 2

INGREDIENTS:

» 2 large bell peppers (any color), halved and seeded
» 1 tablespoon olive oil
» 1/2 small onion, finely chopped
» 1 clove garlic, minced
» 8 ounces lean ground turkey
» 1/2 cup cooked quinoa
» 1/2 cup diced tomatoes
» 1/4 cup shredded mozzarella cheese
» 1 teaspoon dried Italian seasoning
» Salt and pepper, to taste
» Fresh parsley, chopped, for garnish

INSTRUCTIONS:

1. Preheat your oven to 375°F (190°C).
2. Place the bell pepper halves in a baking dish, cut-side up.
3. In a skillet, heat the olive oil over medium heat. Add the chopped onion and minced garlic, and sauté until they are fragrant and softened.
4. Add the ground turkey to the skillet and cook until it is browned and cooked through, breaking it up with a spoon as it cooks.
5. Stir in the cooked quinoa, diced tomatoes, shredded mozzarella cheese, dried Italian seasoning, salt, and pepper. Cook for a few more minutes to heat everything through.
6. Spoon the turkey-quinoa mixture into the bell pepper halves, filling them evenly.
7. Cover the baking dish with foil and bake for about 30 minutes, or until the bell peppers are tender and the filling is heated through.
8. Remove the foil and sprinkle the stuffed bell peppers with fresh parsley before serving.

Nutritional Facts (per serving): Calories: 350; Protein: 30g; Fat: 15g; Carbohydrates: 25g (net); Fiber: 5g.

Tips: Feel free to add additional vegetables or spices to the filling, such as diced zucchini or chili powder. You can also top the stuffed bell peppers with a drizzle of hot sauce or a dollop of Greek yogurt for added flavor.

45. Shrimp Scampi Spaghetti Squash

Preparation Time	**Cooking Time**	**Serving Size**
15 minutes	50 minutes	Serves 2

INGREDIENTS:

- » 1 medium spaghetti squash
- » 1 tablespoon olive oil
- » 1/2 pound shrimp, peeled and deveined
- » 2 cloves garlic, minced
- » Juice of 1 lemon
- » 2 tablespoons butter
- » 2 tablespoons chopped fresh parsley
- » Salt and pepper, to taste
- » Grated Parmesan cheese, for garnish

INSTRUCTIONS:

1. Preheat your oven to 400°F (200°C).
2. Cut the spaghetti squash in half lengthwise and scoop out the seeds. Brush the cut sides with olive oil.
3. Place the spaghetti squash halves, cut-side down, on a baking sheet. Roast them in the preheated oven for about 40 minutes, or until the flesh is tender and can be easily scraped with a fork.
4. While the spaghetti squash is roasting, heat the olive oil in a skillet over medium heat. Add the shrimp and minced garlic, and cook for about 2-3 minutes until the shrimp are pink and cooked through.
5. Squeeze the lemon juice over the shrimp, then add the butter and chopped fresh parsley to the skillet. Stir until the butter is melted and the shrimp are coated in the sauce. Season with salt and pepper to taste.
6. Once the spaghetti squash is cooked, use a fork to scrape the flesh into "noodles."
7. Divide the spaghetti squash noodles between two plates and top them with the shrimp scampi mixture.
8. Garnish with grated Parmesan cheese and serve the shrimp scampi spaghetti squash immediately.

Nutritional Facts (per serving): Calories: 300; Protein: 25g; Fat: 16g; Carbohydrates: 20g (net); Fiber: 4g.

Tips: Feel free to add additional ingredients to the shrimp scampi, such as diced tomatoes or crushed red pepper flakes for a touch of heat. You can also garnish the dish with a squeeze of fresh lemon juice or a sprinkle of chopped fresh basil.

46. Low-Carb Chicken Alfredo

Preparation Time	Cooking Time	Serving Size
10 minutes	20 minutes	Serves 2

INGREDIENTS:

» 8 ounces chicken breast, cut into bite-sized pieces
» Salt and pepper, to taste
» 2 tablespoons butter
» 2 cloves garlic, minced
» 1 cup heavy cream
» 1/2 cup grated Parmesan cheese
» 1/2 teaspoon Italian seasoning
» Fresh parsley, chopped, for garnish
» Low-carb pasta or zucchini noodles, for serving

INSTRUCTIONS:

1. Season the chicken breast pieces with salt and pepper.
2. In a large skillet, melt the butter over medium heat. Add the minced garlic and sauté for about 1 minute until fragrant.
3. Add the chicken breast pieces to the skillet and cook until they are golden brown and cooked through, about 6-8 minutes. Remove the cooked chicken from the skillet and set aside.
4. Reduce the heat to low, then add the heavy cream, grated Parmesan cheese, and Italian seasoning to the skillet. Stir well until the sauce is smooth and creamy.
5. Return the cooked chicken to the skillet and stir to coat the chicken with the Alfredo sauce. Cook for an additional 2-3 minutes until everything is heated through.
6. Serve the low-carb chicken Alfredo over low-carb pasta or zucchini noodles.
7. Garnish with fresh parsley before serving.

Nutritional Facts (per serving): Calories: 450; Protein: 40g; Fat: 30g; Carbohydrates: 6g (net); Fiber: 0g.

Tips: Feel free to add additional vegetables to the Alfredo sauce, such as broccoli florets or sliced mushrooms. You can also top the dish with extra grated Parmesan cheese or a sprinkle of red pepper flakes for added flavor.

47. Spicy Mexican Cauliflower Rice

Preparation Time	Cooking Time	Serving Size
10 minutes	15 minutes	Serves 2

INGREDIENTS:

» 1 small head of cauliflower, grated or finely chopped into rice-like pieces
» 1 tablespoon olive oil
» 1/4 cup diced onion
» 1/4 cup diced bell pepper (any color)
» 1 jalapeño pepper, seeded and minced
» 2 cloves garlic, minced
» 1 teaspoon chili powder
» 1/2 teaspoon ground cumin
» 1/4 teaspoon paprika
» Salt and pepper, to taste
» Fresh cilantro, chopped, for garnish
» Lime wedges, for serving

INSTRUCTIONS:

1. Heat the olive oil in a large skillet over medium heat.
2. Add the diced onion, diced bell pepper, and minced jalapeño pepper to the skillet. Sauté for about 3-4 minutes until the vegetables are softened.
3. Add the minced garlic, chili powder, ground cumin, paprika, salt, and pepper to the skillet. Stir well to combine.
4. Add the grated cauliflower to the skillet and cook for about 5-6 minutes, stirring occasionally, until the cauliflower is tender and cooked through.
5. Taste and adjust the seasonings if necessary.
6. Serve the spicy Mexican cauliflower rice hot, garnished with fresh cilantro. Serve with lime wedges on the side.

Nutritional Facts (per serving): Calories: 150; Protein: 5g; Fat: 7g; Carbohydrates: 12g (net); Fiber: 6g.

Tips: Feel free to add other ingredients to the cauliflower rice, such as diced tomatoes or black beans for added texture and flavor. Adjust the spice level by adding more or less jalapeño pepper according to your preference.

48. Sheet Pan Lemon Pepper Chicken

Preparation Time	Cooking Time	Serving Size
10 minutes	30 minutes	Serves 2

INGREDIENTS:

» 2 boneless, skinless chicken breasts
» Salt and pepper, to taste
» 2 tablespoons olive oil
» 1 tablespoon lemon juice
» 1 teaspoon lemon zest
» 1 teaspoon garlic powder
» 1 teaspoon dried oregano
» 1/2 teaspoon black pepper
» Lemon slices, for garnish
» Fresh parsley, chopped, for garnish

INSTRUCTIONS:

1. Preheat your oven to 425°F (220°C). Line a baking sheet with parchment paper or foil.
2. Season the chicken breasts with salt and pepper on both sides.
3. In a small bowl, whisk together the olive oil, lemon juice, lemon zest, garlic powder, dried oregano, and black pepper.
4. Place the seasoned chicken breasts on the prepared baking sheet. Drizzle the lemon pepper mixture over the chicken, ensuring both sides are coated.
5. Arrange lemon slices on top of the chicken breasts.
6. Bake the chicken in the preheated oven for about 25-30 minutes, or until the chicken is cooked through and reaches an internal temperature of 165°F (74°C).
7. Remove the sheet pan from the oven and let the chicken rest for a few minutes.
8. Garnish with fresh parsley and serve the sheet pan lemon pepper chicken with your favorite side dishes.

Nutritional Facts (per serving): Calories: 300; Protein: 40g; Fat: 14g; Carbohydrates: 2g (net); Fiber: 0g.

Tips: Feel free to add additional herbs or spices to the lemon pepper mixture, such as dried thyme or paprika. Serve the chicken with a side of steamed vegetables or a fresh green salad.

49. Eggplant Parmesan Rollatini

Preparation Time	Cooking Time	Serving Size
30 minutes	45 minutes	Serves 2

INGREDIENTS:

» 1 large eggplant
» Salt, for sprinkling
» 2 tablespoons olive oil
» 1 cup ricotta cheese
» 1/4 cup grated Parmesan cheese
» 1/4 cup chopped fresh basil
» 1 clove garlic, minced
» 1 cup marinara sauce
» 1/2 cup shredded mozzarella cheese
» Fresh basil leaves, for garnish

INSTRUCTIONS:

1. Preheat your oven to 375°F (190°C).
2. Slice the eggplant lengthwise into thin, 1/4-inch thick slices. Sprinkle salt over both sides of each slice and let them sit for about 10 minutes. This will help remove excess moisture from the eggplant.
3. Rinse the eggplant slices under cold water to remove the salt. Pat them dry with paper towels.
4. Heat the olive oil in a large skillet over medium-high heat. Add the eggplant slices and cook for about 2 minutes per side until lightly browned and softened. Remove from the skillet and set aside.
5. In a bowl, combine the ricotta cheese, grated Parmesan cheese, chopped fresh basil, and minced garlic. Mix well.
6. Spread a spoonful of marinara sauce on each eggplant slice. Spoon some of the ricotta mixture onto one end of each eggplant slice, then roll it up.
7. Place the eggplant rollatini seam-side down in a baking dish. Pour the remaining marinara sauce over the rollatini.
8. Sprinkle shredded mozzarella cheese over the top.
9. Bake in the preheated oven for about 25-30 minutes, or until the cheese is melted and bubbly.
10. Remove from the oven and let it cool slightly. Garnish with fresh basil leaves before serving.

Nutritional Facts (per serving): Calories: 350; Protein: 15g; Fat: 20g; Carbohydrates: 25g (net); Fiber: 8g.

Tips: Feel free to add additional herbs or spices to the ricotta mixture, such as dried oregano or red pepper flakes. Serve the eggplant Parmesan rollatini with a side of mixed greens or a simple pasta dish.

50. Grilled Portobello Mushroom Burgers

Preparation Time	Cooking Time	Serving Size
15 minutes	10 minutes	Serves 2

INGREDIENTS:

» 2 large portobello mushroom caps
» 2 tablespoons balsamic vinegar
» 2 tablespoons olive oil
» 2 cloves garlic, minced
» Salt and pepper, to taste
» 4 slices of your favorite burger buns
» Burger toppings of your choice (lettuce, tomato, onion, etc.)

INSTRUCTIONS:

1. Preheat your grill or grill pan to medium heat.
2. Remove the stems from the portobello mushroom caps and wipe them clean with a damp paper towel.
3. In a small bowl, whisk together the balsamic vinegar, olive oil, minced garlic, salt, and pepper.
4. Brush the marinade mixture over both sides of the portobello mushroom caps.
5. Place the mushroom caps on the grill or grill pan, gill-side down. Cook for about 4-5 minutes per side until they are tender and juicy.
6. Toast the burger buns on the grill for a minute or two, if desired.
7. Assemble your grilled portobello mushroom burgers by placing the cooked mushroom caps on the bottom bun. Top with your favorite burger toppings.
8. Serve the burgers immediately.

Nutritional Facts (per serving): Calories: 250; Protein: 5g; Fat: 12g; Carbohydrates: 30g (net); Fiber: 3g.

Tips: Feel free to add additional seasonings or spices to the marinade, such as dried thyme or smoked paprika. You can also add your favorite cheese or sauce to the burger for added flavor.

Dinner High Carb

51. Vegan Chickpea Curry with Brown Rice

Preparation Time	**Cooking Time**	**Serving Size**
15 minutes	25 minutes	Serves 2

INGREDIENTS:

» 1 tablespoon coconut oil
» 1 small onion, diced
» 2 cloves garlic, minced
» 1 tablespoon grated fresh ginger
» 1 tablespoon curry powder
» 1/2 teaspoon turmeric powder
» 1/2 teaspoon cumin powder
» 1 can (15 ounces) chickpeas, drained and rinsed
» 1 can (14 ounces) diced tomatoes
» 1 can (13.5 ounces) coconut milk
» 1 cup vegetable broth
» 2 cups cooked brown rice
» Fresh cilantro, chopped, for garnish
» Lime wedges, for serving

INSTRUCTIONS:

1. Heat the coconut oil in a large skillet or pot over medium heat.
2. Add the diced onion to the skillet and sauté until it becomes translucent and lightly golden.
3. Stir in the minced garlic, grated ginger, curry powder, turmeric powder, and cumin powder. Cook for about 1 minute until fragrant.
4. Add the drained and rinsed chickpeas, diced tomatoes (with their juices), coconut milk, and vegetable broth to the skillet. Stir well to combine.
5. Bring the mixture to a simmer and let it cook for about 15-20 minutes, stirring occasionally, until the flavors are well combined and the curry has thickened slightly.
6. Serve the vegan chickpea curry over cooked brown rice.
7. Garnish with fresh cilantro and serve with lime wedges on the side.

Nutritional Facts (per serving): Calories: 450; Protein: 12g; Fat: 20g; Carbohydrates: 55g (net); Fiber: 12g.

Tips: Feel free to customize the curry by adding more vegetables like spinach or bell peppers. Adjust the spices according to your preference for a milder or spicier curry. Enjoy this delicious and nutritious vegan dish!

52. Loaded Veggie Pizza

Preparation Time	Cooking Time	Serving Size
20 minutes	15 minutes	Serves 2

INGREDIENTS:

- » 1 pre-made pizza dough (store-bought or homemade)
- » 1/4 cup pizza sauce
- » 1 cup shredded vegan cheese (such as vegan mozzarella or cheddar)
- » 1/4 cup sliced bell peppers
- » 1/4 cup sliced red onions
- » 1/4 cup sliced mushrooms
- » 1/4 cup sliced black olives
- » 1/4 cup chopped fresh tomatoes
- » 1/4 cup fresh basil leaves, torn
- » Crushed red pepper flakes, for optional heat

INSTRUCTIONS:

1. Preheat your oven to the temperature specified on the pizza dough package or your homemade dough recipe.
2. Roll out the pizza dough on a lightly floured surface to your desired thickness and shape.
3. Transfer the rolled-out dough to a pizza stone or baking sheet lined with parchment paper.
4. Spread the pizza sauce evenly over the dough, leaving a small border around the edges.
5. Sprinkle the shredded vegan cheese over the sauce.
6. Arrange the sliced bell peppers, red onions, mushrooms, black olives, and chopped tomatoes over the cheese.
7. Bake the pizza in the preheated oven for about 12-15 minutes, or until the crust is golden brown and the cheese is melted and bubbly.
8. Remove the pizza from the oven and let it cool slightly.
9. Sprinkle the torn fresh basil leaves over the pizza and, if desired, add crushed red pepper flakes for extra heat.
10. Slice the loaded veggie pizza and serve hot.

Nutritional Facts (per serving): Calories: 350; Protein: 10g; Fat: 8g; Carbohydrates: 55g (net); Fiber: 8g.

Tips: Feel free to add additional vegetables or toppings to the pizza based on your preference. You can also drizzle a bit of extra virgin olive oil or balsamic glaze over the pizza before serving for added flavor. Enjoy this tasty and colorful loaded veggie pizza!

53. Quinoa Stuffed Bell Peppers

Preparation Time	Cooking Time	Serving Size
15 minutes	40 minutes	Serves 2

INGREDIENTS:

- » 2 bell peppers (any color), tops removed and seeds removed
- » 1 tablespoon olive oil
- » 1 small onion, diced
- » 2 cloves garlic, minced
- » 1 cup cooked quinoa
- » 1 cup black beans, drained and rinsed
- » 1 cup diced tomatoes
- » 1/2 cup corn kernels
- » 1 teaspoon chili powder
- » 1/2 teaspoon cumin
- » Salt and pepper, to taste
- » Fresh cilantro, chopped, for garnish

INSTRUCTIONS:

1. Preheat your oven to 375°F (190°C).
2. In a large pot, bring water to a boil. Add the bell peppers and blanch them for about 5 minutes until slightly softened. Drain and set aside.
3. Heat the olive oil in a skillet over medium heat. Add the diced onion and minced garlic, and sauté until they are fragrant and softened.
4. Stir in the cooked quinoa, black beans, diced tomatoes, corn kernels, chili powder, cumin, salt, and pepper. Cook for a few more minutes to heat everything through.
5. Stuff the bell peppers with the quinoa mixture and place them upright in a baking dish.
6. Bake in the preheated oven for about 25-30 minutes until the bell peppers are tender and the filling is heated through.
7. Remove from the oven and let them cool slightly. Garnish with fresh cilantro before serving.

Nutritional Facts (per serving): Calories: 350; Protein: 12g; Fat: 6g; Carbohydrates: 65g (net); Fiber: 14g.

Tips: Feel free to add additional vegetables or spices to the quinoa filling, such as diced zucchini or paprika. Serve the quinoa stuffed bell peppers with a side of salsa or a green salad for a complete meal.

54. Lemon Herb Pasta with Shrimp

Preparation Time	**Cooking Time**	**Serving Size**
15 minutes	15 minutes	Serves 2

INGREDIENTS:

» 6 ounces linguine or your favorite pasta
» 1 tablespoon olive oil
» 1/2 pound shrimp, peeled and deveined
» Salt and pepper, to taste
» 2 cloves garlic, minced
» Zest of 1 lemon
» Juice of 1 lemon
» 2 tablespoons butter
» 2 tablespoons chopped fresh parsley
» Grated Parmesan cheese, for serving

INSTRUCTIONS:

1. Cook the linguine according to the package instructions until al dente. Drain and set aside.
2. Heat the olive oil in a skillet over medium heat. Add the shrimp and season with salt and pepper. Cook for about 2-3 minutes per side until they are pink and cooked through. Remove from the skillet and set aside.
3. In the same skillet, add the minced garlic, lemon zest, and lemon juice. Sauté for about 1 minute until fragrant.
4. Add the cooked linguine to the skillet and toss well to coat the pasta with the lemon garlic mixture.
5. Add the cooked shrimp back to the skillet. Stir in the butter and chopped fresh parsley. Cook for an additional minute until everything is heated through and well combined.
6. Serve the lemon herb pasta with shrimp hot, garnished with grated Parmesan cheese.

Nutritional Facts (per serving): Calories: 400; Protein: 25g; Fat: 12g; Carbohydrates: 50g (net); Fiber: 4g.

Tips: Feel free to add additional herbs or spices to the pasta, such as dried basil or red pepper flakes. You can also add sautéed vegetables like cherry tomatoes or baby spinach for added color and flavor.

55. Hearty Vegetarian Lasagna

Preparation Time	Cooking Time	Serving Size
30 minutes	50 minutes	Serves 2

INGREDIENTS:

» 6 lasagna noodles
» 2 cups marinara sauce
» 1 cup ricotta cheese
» 1 cup shredded mozzarella cheese
» 1/2 cup grated Parmesan cheese
» 1 cup chopped fresh spinach
» 1/2 cup sliced mushrooms
» 1/2 cup diced bell peppers
» 1/2 cup diced onions
» 2 cloves garlic, minced
» 1/2 teaspoon dried oregano
» 1/2 teaspoon dried basil
» Salt and pepper, to taste
» Fresh basil leaves, for garnish

INSTRUCTIONS:

1. Preheat your oven to 375°F (190°C).
2. Cook the lasagna noodles according to the package instructions until al dente. Drain and set aside.
3. In a skillet, sauté the minced garlic, diced onions, sliced mushrooms, and diced bell peppers until they are softened.
4. Add the chopped fresh spinach to the skillet and cook until it wilts.
5. In a bowl, combine the ricotta cheese, dried oregano, dried basil, salt, and pepper.
6. Spread a thin layer of marinara sauce on the bottom of a baking dish.
7. Layer 2 lasagna noodles over the sauce.
8. Spread half of the ricotta cheese mixture over the noodles.
9. Sprinkle half of the sautéed vegetables over the ricotta layer.
10. Repeat the layers with marinara sauce, lasagna noodles, remaining ricotta cheese mixture, and remaining sautéed vegetables.
11. Top the lasagna with marinara sauce, shredded mozzarella cheese, and grated Parmesan cheese.
12. Cover the baking dish with foil and bake in the preheated oven for about 30 minutes.
13. Remove the foil and bake for an additional 10-15 minutes until the cheese is melted and bubbly.
14. Remove from the oven and let it cool slightly. Garnish with fresh basil leaves before serving.

Nutritional Facts (per serving): Calories: 500; Protein: 25g; Fat: 18g; Carbohydrates: 55g (net); Fiber: 6g.

Tips: Feel free to add other vegetables or ingredients to the lasagna layers, such as zucchini slices or vegan cheese for a dairy-free option. Serve the hearty vegetarian lasagna with a side of garlic bread or a fresh green salad.

56. Sweet Potato and Black Bean Chili

Preparation Time	Cooking Time	Serving Size
15 minutes	30 minutes	Serves 2

INGREDIENTS:

» 1 tablespoon olive oil
» 1 small onion, diced
» 2 cloves garlic, minced
» 1 small sweet potato, peeled and diced
» 1 can (14 ounces) diced tomatoes
» 1 can (14 ounces) black beans, drained and rinsed
» 1 cup vegetable broth
» 1 tablespoon chili powder
» 1 teaspoon ground cumin
» 1/2 teaspoon paprika
» Salt and pepper, to taste
» Fresh cilantro, chopped, for garnish
» Sour cream or Greek yogurt, for serving (optional)

INSTRUCTIONS:

1. Heat the olive oil in a large pot over medium heat. Add the diced onion and minced garlic, and sauté until they are fragrant and softened.
2. Add the diced sweet potato to the pot and cook for about 5 minutes until it starts to soften.
3. Stir in the diced tomatoes, black beans, vegetable broth, chili powder, ground cumin, paprika, salt, and pepper. Mix well to combine.
4. Bring the mixture to a boil, then reduce the heat to low. Cover the pot and let the chili simmer for about 20-25 minutes, stirring occasionally, until the sweet potatoes are tender.
5. Taste and adjust the seasonings if necessary.
6. Serve the sweet potato and black bean chili hot, garnished with fresh cilantro. Top with a dollop of sour cream or Greek yogurt if desired.

Nutritional Facts (per serving): Calories: 350; Protein: 12g; Fat: 6g; Carbohydrates: 65g (net); Fiber: 14g.

Tips: Feel free to customize the chili by adding additional vegetables like bell peppers or corn kernels. You can also adjust the spiciness by adding more chili powder or a dash of hot sauce. Enjoy this hearty and flavorful sweet potato and black bean chili!

57. Moroccan Lentil Stew

Preparation Time	Cooking Time	Serving Size
15 minutes	35 minutes	Serves 2

INGREDIENTS:

» 1 tablespoon olive oil
» 1 small onion, diced
» 2 cloves garlic, minced
» 1 carrot, diced
» 1 small sweet potato, peeled and diced
» 1 cup dried red lentils
» 1 can (14 ounces) diced tomatoes
» 2 cups vegetable broth
» 1 teaspoon ground cumin
» 1 teaspoon ground coriander
» 1/2 teaspoon ground cinnamon
» 1/2 teaspoon paprika
» Salt and pepper, to taste
» Fresh parsley, chopped, for garnish
» Lemon wedges, for serving

INSTRUCTIONS:

1. Heat the olive oil in a large pot over medium heat. Add the diced onion and minced garlic, and sauté until they are fragrant and softened.
2. Add the diced carrot and sweet potato to the pot, and cook for about 5 minutes until they start to soften.
3. Rinse the red lentils under cold water and add them to the pot. Stir well to combine.
4. Pour in the diced tomatoes and vegetable broth. Add the ground cumin, ground coriander, ground cinnamon, paprika, salt, and pepper. Mix well to combine.
5. Bring the mixture to a boil, then reduce the heat to low. Cover the pot and let the lentil stew simmer for about 25-30 minutes, or until the lentils and vegetables are tender.
6. Taste and adjust the seasonings if necessary.
7. Serve the Moroccan lentil stew hot, garnished with fresh parsley. Squeeze a lemon wedge over each serving before eating.

Nutritional Facts (per serving): Calories: 350; Protein: 16g; Fat: 6g; Carbohydrates: 60g (net); Fiber: 16g.

Tips: Feel free to add additional spices or herbs to the lentil stew, such as turmeric or smoked paprika. Serve the Moroccan lentil stew with a side of couscous or warm crusty bread for a complete and satisfying meal.

58. Teriyaki Chicken and Rice Bowl

Preparation Time	Cooking Time	Serving Size
15 minutes	20 minutes	Serves 2

INGREDIENTS:

» 2 boneless, skinless chicken breasts, sliced into thin strips
» Salt and pepper, to taste
» 2 tablespoons soy sauce
» 2 tablespoons honey or maple syrup
» 1 tablespoon rice vinegar
» 1 tablespoon sesame oil
» 1 clove garlic, minced
» 1 teaspoon grated fresh ginger
» 2 cups cooked brown rice
» 1 cup steamed broccoli florets
» 1/2 cup sliced carrots
» 1/2 cup sliced bell peppers
» Sesame seeds, for garnish
» Green onions, sliced, for garnish

INSTRUCTIONS:

1. Season the chicken breast strips with salt and pepper.
2. In a small bowl, whisk together the soy sauce, honey or maple syrup, rice vinegar, sesame oil, minced garlic, and grated ginger.
3. Heat a non-stick skillet or wok over medium-high heat. Add the chicken breast strips and cook for about 5-6 minutes until they are browned and cooked through.
4. Pour the teriyaki sauce over the cooked chicken, stirring well to coat. Cook for an additional minute to heat the sauce through.
5. Divide the cooked brown rice between two bowls. Top with the teriyaki chicken, steamed broccoli florets, sliced carrots, and sliced bell peppers.
6. Garnish with sesame seeds and sliced green onions.
7. Serve the teriyaki chicken and rice bowl hot.

Nutritional Facts (per serving): Calories: 400; Protein: 30g; Fat: 8g; Carbohydrates: 55g (net); Fiber: 6g.

Tips: Feel free to add additional vegetables or toppings to the rice bowl, such as sliced mushrooms or snow peas. You can also drizzle extra teriyaki sauce over the bowl for added flavor. Enjoy this delicious and satisfying teriyaki chicken and rice bowl!

59. Butternut Squash Mac and Cheese

Preparation Time	**Cooking Time**	**Serving Size**
20 minutes	40 minutes	Serves 2

INGREDIENTS:

» 8 ounces elbow macaroni or your favorite pasta
» 2 cups cubed butternut squash
» 1 tablespoon olive oil
» 1 small onion, diced
» 2 cloves garlic, minced
» 1 cup vegetable broth
» 1/2 cup unsweetened almond milk or your preferred milk
» 1 cup shredded cheddar cheese or your favorite cheese
» 1/4 cup grated Parmesan cheese
» 1/2 teaspoon dried thyme
» Salt and pepper, to taste
» Fresh parsley, chopped, for garnish

INSTRUCTIONS:

1. Cook the elbow macaroni according to the package instructions until al dente. Drain and set aside.
2. In a steamer basket or microwave-safe dish, steam the cubed butternut squash until it becomes tender. Set aside.
3. Heat the olive oil in a skillet over medium heat. Add the diced onion and minced garlic, and sauté until they are fragrant and softened.
4. In a blender or food processor, combine the steamed butternut squash, sautéed onion and garlic, vegetable broth, almond milk, shredded cheddar cheese, grated Parmesan cheese, dried thyme, salt, and pepper. Blend until smooth and creamy.
5. Pour the butternut squash sauce over the cooked macaroni. Stir well to coat the pasta with the sauce.
6. Cook the mac and cheese over low heat for a few minutes until everything is heated through.
7. Serve the butternut squash mac and cheese hot, garnished with fresh parsley.

Nutritional Facts (per serving): Calories: 450; Protein: 18g; Fat: 15g; Carbohydrates: 60g (net); Fiber: 6g.

Tips: Feel free to add additional spices or herbs to the butternut squash sauce, such as nutmeg or sage. For a crispy topping, sprinkle breadcrumbs or crushed crackers over the mac and cheese before baking it in the oven. Enjoy this creamy and flavorful butternut squash mac and cheese!

60. Greek Orzo with Grilled Vegetables

Preparation Time	**Cooking Time**	**Serving Size**
20 minutes	15 minutes	Serves 2

INGREDIENTS:

» 1 cup orzo pasta
» 2 tablespoons olive oil, divided
» 1 small eggplant, sliced into rounds
» 1 small zucchini, sliced into rounds
» 1 red bell pepper, sliced into strips
» 1 small red onion, sliced into rings
» Salt and pepper, to taste
» 1/2 cup cherry tomatoes, halved
» 1/4 cup sliced Kalamata olives
» 2 tablespoons chopped fresh parsley
» 2 tablespoons crumbled feta cheese
» Lemon wedges, for serving

INSTRUCTIONS:

1. Cook the orzo pasta according to the package instructions until al dente. Drain and set aside.
2. Preheat a grill or grill pan over medium-high heat.
3. Brush the sliced eggplant, zucchini, red bell pepper, and red onion with olive oil. Season with salt and pepper.
4. Grill the vegetables for a few minutes on each side until they are charred and tender. Remove from the grill and let them cool slightly. Chop the grilled vegetables into bite-sized pieces.
5. In a large bowl, combine the cooked orzo pasta, chopped grilled vegetables, cherry tomatoes, sliced Kalamata olives, chopped fresh parsley, and crumbled feta cheese.
6. Drizzle the remaining olive oil over the orzo mixture. Season with additional salt and pepper, if desired.
7. Toss everything together until well combined.
8. Serve the Greek orzo with grilled vegetables at room temperature or chilled, with lemon wedges on the side.

Nutritional Facts (per serving): Calories: 400; Protein: 10g; Fat: 15g; Carbohydrates: 60g (net); Fiber: 6g.

Tips: Feel free to add other vegetables or herbs to the orzo salad, such as cucumber or fresh mint. You can also squeeze fresh lemon juice over the salad before serving for an extra burst of flavor. Enjoy this refreshing and satisfying Greek orzo with grilled vegetables!

61. Avocado Deviled Eggs

Preparation Time	Cooking Time	Serving Size
15 minutes	10 minutes	Serves 2

INGREDIENTS:

» 4 large eggs
» 1 ripe avocado
» 1 tablespoon mayonnaise
» 1 tablespoon Dijon mustard
» 1 tablespoon fresh lemon juice
» Salt and pepper, to taste
» Paprika, for garnish
» Fresh chives, chopped, for garnish

INSTRUCTIONS:

1. Place the eggs in a saucepan and cover them with water. Bring the water to a boil over high heat.
2. Once the water reaches a rolling boil, reduce the heat to low and let the eggs simmer for about 10 minutes.
3. Remove the eggs from the heat and transfer them to a bowl of ice water. Let them cool for a few minutes.
4. Peel the cooled hard-boiled eggs and slice them in half lengthwise. Carefully remove the yolks and transfer them to a mixing bowl.
5. Add the ripe avocado, mayonnaise, Dijon mustard, fresh lemon juice, salt, and pepper to the mixing bowl with the egg yolks.
6. Mash the ingredients together until smooth and well combined.
7. Spoon the avocado and egg yolk mixture into the egg white halves, evenly distributing it among them.
8. Sprinkle each deviled egg with a pinch of paprika and chopped fresh chives for garnish.
9. Serve the avocado deviled eggs chilled.

Nutritional Facts (per serving): Calories: 200; Protein: 12g; Fat: 15g; Carbohydrates: 5g (net); Fiber: 4g.

Tips: Feel free to add additional spices or herbs to the avocado and egg yolk mixture, such as garlic powder or chopped fresh cilantro. You can also experiment with different garnishes like crispy bacon bits or smoked paprika. Enjoy these creamy and flavorful avocado deviled eggs!

62. Smoked Salmon Cucumber Bites

Preparation Time	**Cooking Time**	**Serving Size**
10 minutes	None (No cooking required)	Serves 2

INGREDIENTS:

- » 1 English cucumber
- » 4 ounces smoked salmon
- » 4 tablespoons cream cheese
- » Fresh dill, for garnish
- » Lemon zest, for garnish

INSTRUCTIONS:

1. Slice the English cucumber into thin rounds, about 1/4 inch thick.
2. Arrange the cucumber slices on a serving platter or individual plates.
3. Spread a thin layer of cream cheese onto each cucumber slice.
4. Cut the smoked salmon into small pieces that will fit on top of the cucumber slices.
5. Place a piece of smoked salmon on each cucumber slice, on top of the cream cheese.
6. Garnish the smoked salmon cucumber bites with fresh dill and a sprinkle of lemon zest.
7. Serve the bites immediately.

Nutritional Facts (per serving): Calories: 180; Protein: 15g; Fat: 10g; Carbohydrates: 5g (net); Fiber: 1g.

Tips: Feel free to add additional toppings or flavors to the smoked salmon cucumber bites, such as capers or a squeeze of fresh lemon juice. You can also use flavored cream cheese, such as dill or garlic herb, for extra taste. Enjoy these light and refreshing smoked salmon cucumber bites!

63. Spicy Roasted Almonds

Preparation Time	**Cooking Time**	**Serving Size**
5 minutes	15 minutes	Serves 2

INGREDIENTS:

- » 1 cup raw almonds
- » 1 tablespoon olive oil
- » 1/2 teaspoon smoked paprika
- » 1/4 teaspoon cayenne pepper (adjust to taste)
- » 1/2 teaspoon garlic powder
- » 1/2 teaspoon sea salt

INSTRUCTIONS:

1. Preheat your oven to 350°F (175°C).
2. In a bowl, combine the raw almonds, olive oil, smoked paprika, cayenne pepper, garlic powder, and sea salt. Toss well to coat the almonds evenly with the spice mixture.
3. Spread the seasoned almonds in a single layer on a baking sheet.
4. Roast the almonds in the preheated oven for about 12-15 minutes, stirring halfway through, until they are golden brown and fragrant.
5. Remove the almonds from the oven and let them cool completely.
6. Serve the spicy roasted almonds as a snack or add them to salads or trail mixes.

Nutritional Facts (per serving): Calories: 200; Protein: 8g; Fat: 18g; Carbohydrates: 7g (net); Fiber: 4g.

Tips: Feel free to adjust the level of spiciness by adding more or less cayenne pepper. You can also experiment with different spices or herbs, such as chili powder or rosemary, to suit your taste preferences. Enjoy these crunchy and flavorful spicy roasted almonds!

64. Mediterranean Olives and Feta Skewers

Preparation Time	Cooking Time	Serving Size
10 minutes	None (No cooking required)	Serves 2

INGREDIENTS:

» 1 cup mixed Mediterranean olives (such as Kalamata and green olives)
» 4 ounces feta cheese, cut into cubes
» 2 tablespoons extra virgin olive oil
» 1 teaspoon dried oregano
» Fresh parsley, chopped, for garnish

INSTRUCTIONS:

1. Thread the mixed Mediterranean olives and feta cheese cubes onto skewers, alternating them.
2. Drizzle the skewers with extra virgin olive oil and sprinkle them with dried oregano.
3. Garnish with chopped fresh parsley.
4. Serve the Mediterranean olives and feta skewers as an appetizer or part of a mezze platter.

Nutritional Facts (per serving): Calories: 200; Protein: 8g; Fat: 16g; Carbohydrates: 5g (net); Fiber: 1g.

Tips: Feel free to add additional ingredients to the skewers, such as cherry tomatoes or marinated artichoke hearts. Serve them with warm pita bread or toasted baguette slices for a complete Mediterranean-inspired appetizer.

65. Veggie Dippers with Hummus

Preparation Time	Cooking Time	Serving Size
10 minutes	None (No cooking required)	Serves 2

INGREDIENTS:

» Assorted vegetables for dipping (such as carrot sticks, celery sticks, cucumber slices, and bell pepper strips)
» 1 cup hummus (store-bought or homemade)
» Fresh parsley, chopped, for garnish

INSTRUCTIONS:

1. Wash and cut the assorted vegetables into sticks and slices.
2. Arrange the vegetable dippers on a serving platter or individual plates.
3. Place a bowl of hummus in the center of the platter or on each plate.
4. Garnish the hummus with chopped fresh parsley.
5. Serve the veggie dippers with hummus as a healthy and refreshing snack or appetizer.

Nutritional Facts (per serving): Calories: 150; Protein: 6g; Fat: 10g; Carbohydrates: 12g (net); Fiber: 6g.

Tips: Feel free to customize the assortment of vegetables based on your preferences. You can also try different flavors of hummus, such as roasted red pepper or garlic, for variety. Enjoy these crunchy and nutritious veggie dippers with creamy hummus!

66. Greek Yogurt Ranch Dip with Veggies

Preparation Time	Cooking Time	Serving Size
10 minutes	None (No cooking required)	Serves 2

INGREDIENTS:

» 1 cup Greek yogurt
» 2 tablespoons fresh dill, chopped
» 2 tablespoons fresh parsley, chopped
» 1 tablespoon fresh chives, chopped
» 1 clove garlic, minced
» 1/2 teaspoon onion powder
» 1/2 teaspoon dried dill
» 1/2 teaspoon dried parsley
» Salt and pepper, to taste
» Assorted vegetables for dipping (such as carrot sticks, celery sticks, cucumber slices, and bell pepper strips)

INSTRUCTIONS:

1. In a bowl, combine the Greek yogurt, fresh dill, fresh parsley, fresh chives, minced garlic, onion powder, dried dill, dried parsley, salt, and pepper. Mix well to combine.
2. Cover the bowl and refrigerate the Greek yogurt ranch dip for at least 30 minutes to allow the flavors to meld together.
3. Wash and cut the assorted vegetables into sticks and slices.
4. Arrange the vegetable dippers on a serving platter or individual plates.
5. Serve the Greek yogurt ranch dip alongside the veggie dippers as a healthy and tangy dip.

Nutritional Facts (per serving): Calories: 120; Protein: 12g; Fat: 4g; Carbohydrates: 10g (net); Fiber: 2g.

Tips: Feel free to adjust the herb and spice quantities based on your taste preferences. You can also add a squeeze of fresh lemon juice for extra brightness. Enjoy this creamy and flavorful Greek yogurt ranch dip with a variety of fresh vegetables!

67. Keto Coconut Macaroons

Preparation Time	Cooking Time	Serving Size
10 minutes	15 minutes	Makes about 12 macaroons

INGREDIENTS:

» 2 cups unsweetened shredded coconut
» 3/4 cup keto-friendly sweetener (such as erythritol or monk fruit)
» 4 egg whites
» 1/2 teaspoon vanilla extract
» Pinch of salt

INSTRUCTIONS:

1. Preheat your oven to 325°F (165°C). Line a baking sheet with parchment paper.
2. In a mixing bowl, combine the unsweetened shredded coconut, keto-friendly sweetener, egg whites, vanilla extract, and pinch of salt. Mix well until all the ingredients are evenly combined.
3. Using a cookie scoop or tablespoon, portion out the coconut mixture onto the prepared baking sheet, forming small mounds or domes.
4. Bake the macaroons in the preheated oven for about 15 minutes or until they turn golden brown around the edges.
5. Remove the macaroons from the oven and let them cool on the baking sheet for a few minutes. Then transfer them to a wire rack to cool completely.
6. Serve the keto coconut macaroons as a delightful low-carb and gluten-free treat.

Nutritional Facts (per macaroon): Calories: 90; Protein: 1g; Fat: 8g; Carbohydrates: 3g (net); Fiber: 2g.

Tips: For added variety, you can dip the bottom of the cooled macaroons in melted dark chocolate and let them set before serving. Enjoy these delicious and keto-friendly coconut macaroons as a guilt-free dessert!

68. Mini Bell Pepper Nachos

Preparation Time	Cooking Time	Serving Size
10 minutes	10 minutes	Serves 2

INGREDIENTS:

» 6 mini bell peppers, halved and seeds removed
» 1/2 cup shredded cheddar cheese or your preferred cheese
» 1/4 cup diced tomatoes
» 1/4 cup diced red onions
» 2 tablespoons sliced black olives
» 2 tablespoons chopped fresh cilantro
» Guacamole and sour cream, for serving (optional)

INSTRUCTIONS:

1. Preheat your oven to 400°F (200°C). Line a baking sheet with parchment paper.
2. Place the halved mini bell peppers on the prepared baking sheet, cut-side up.
3. Fill each pepper half with a sprinkle of shredded cheddar cheese, diced tomatoes, diced red onions, and sliced black olives.
4. Bake the mini bell pepper nachos in the preheated oven for about 8-10 minutes or until the cheese is melted and bubbly.
5. Remove the nachos from the oven and let them cool for a minute. Sprinkle fresh cilantro over the top.
6. Serve the mini bell pepper nachos hot, with guacamole and sour cream on the side for dipping if desired.

Nutritional Facts (per serving): Calories: 180; Protein: 8g; Fat: 13g; Carbohydrates: 9g (net); Fiber: 2g.

Tips: Feel free to customize the toppings on the mini bell pepper nachos according to your preferences. You can add sliced jalapeños for an extra kick or cooked ground meat for a heartier version. Enjoy these colorful and flavorful nachos as a healthier alternative to traditional nachos!

69. Zucchini Chips with Guacamole

Preparation Time	Cooking Time	Serving Size
15 minutes	20 minutes	Serves 2

INGREDIENTS:

» 2 medium zucchini, sliced into thin rounds
» 2 tablespoons olive oil
» 1 teaspoon garlic powder
» 1/2 teaspoon paprika
» Salt and pepper, to taste
» Guacamole, for serving

INSTRUCTIONS:

1. Preheat your oven to 375°F (190°C). Line a baking sheet with parchment paper.
2. In a large bowl, combine the sliced zucchini, olive oil, garlic powder, paprika, salt, and pepper. Toss well to evenly coat the zucchini slices.
3. Arrange the seasoned zucchini slices in a single layer on the prepared baking sheet.
4. Bake the zucchini chips in the preheated oven for about 15-20 minutes, flipping them halfway through, until they turn golden brown and crispy.
5. Remove the chips from the oven and let them cool for a few minutes.
6. Serve the zucchini chips with a side of guacamole for dipping.

Nutritional Facts (per serving): Calories: 150; Protein: 2g; Fat: 13g; Carbohydrates: 7g (net); Fiber: 2g.

Tips: Feel free to adjust the seasoning on the zucchini chips based on your taste preferences. You can also sprinkle grated Parmesan cheese or nutritional yeast over the chips before baking for added flavor. Enjoy these crispy and nutritious zucchini chips with creamy guacamole!

70. Buffalo Chicken Celery Sticks

Preparation Time	Cooking Time	Serving Size
15 minutes	15 minutes	Serves 2

INGREDIENTS:

» 2 large celery stalks, washed and trimmed
» 1 cup cooked shredded chicken breast
» 2 tablespoons hot sauce (such as Frank's RedHot)
» 2 tablespoons unsalted butter, melted
» 1/4 teaspoon garlic powder
» Salt and pepper, to taste
» Blue cheese or ranch dressing, for drizzling

INSTRUCTIONS:

1. Cut the celery stalks into smaller sticks, approximately 3-4 inches long.
2. In a bowl, combine the shredded chicken, hot sauce, melted butter, garlic powder, salt, and pepper. Mix well to evenly coat the chicken with the buffalo sauce.
3. Fill each celery stick with a spoonful of the buffalo chicken mixture.
4. Drizzle blue cheese or ranch dressing over the top of the celery sticks.
5. Serve the buffalo chicken celery sticks as a spicy and low-carb appetizer or snack.

Nutritional Facts (per serving): Calories: 180; Protein: 20g; Fat: 10g; Carbohydrates: 2g (net); Fiber: 1g.

Tips: Feel free to adjust the spiciness of the buffalo chicken mixture by adding more or less hot sauce. You can also sprinkle crumbled blue cheese or chopped green onions over the top for extra flavor. Enjoy these tangy and protein-packed buffalo chicken celery sticks!

Snacks High Carb

71. Baked Sweet Potato Fries

Preparation Time	Cooking Time	Serving Size
10 minutes	30 minutes	Serves 2

INGREDIENTS:

» 2 medium sweet potatoes
» 2 tablespoons olive oil
» 1 teaspoon paprika
» 1/2 teaspoon garlic powder
» 1/2 teaspoon onion powder
» 1/4 teaspoon salt
» 1/4 teaspoon black pepper

INSTRUCTIONS:

1. Preheat your oven to 425°F (220°C). Line a baking sheet with parchment paper.
2. Wash and peel the sweet potatoes. Cut them into long, thin strips to resemble fries.
3. In a large bowl, toss the sweet potato strips with olive oil, paprika, garlic powder, onion powder, salt, and black pepper. Make sure the fries are evenly coated with the seasoning.
4. Spread the seasoned sweet potato fries in a single layer on the prepared baking sheet.
5. Bake the fries in the preheated oven for about 25-30 minutes, flipping them halfway through, until they turn golden brown and crispy.
6. Remove the fries from the oven and let them cool for a few minutes.
7. Serve the baked sweet potato fries as a healthier alternative to traditional fries, with your favorite dipping sauce on the side.

Nutritional Facts (per serving): Calories: 180; Protein: 2g; Fat: 8g; Carbohydrates: 26g (net); Fiber: 4g.

Tips: For added flavor, you can sprinkle grated Parmesan cheese or chopped fresh herbs, such as rosemary or parsley, over the fries before baking. Enjoy these crispy and guilt-free baked sweet potato fries!

72. Energy-Boosting Trail Mix

Preparation Time	Cooking Time	Serving Size
5 minutes	None (No cooking required)	Makes about 2 cups

INGREDIENTS:

» 1 cup raw almonds
» 1/2 cup dried cranberries
» 1/2 cup unsweetened coconut flakes
» 1/4 cup dark chocolate chips or chunks
» 1/4 cup pumpkin seeds
» 1/4 cup cashews

INSTRUCTIONS:

1. In a bowl, combine the raw almonds, dried cranberries, unsweetened coconut flakes, dark chocolate chips or chunks, pumpkin seeds, and cashews.
2. Toss the ingredients together until they are well mixed.
3. Transfer the energy-boosting trail mix to an airtight container for storage.
4. Serve the trail mix as a nutritious and convenient snack to keep you energized throughout the day.

Nutritional Facts (per serving, about 1/4 cup): Calories: 160; Protein: 4g; Fat: 12g; Carbohydrates: 11g (net); Fiber: 3g.

Tips: Feel free to customize the trail mix by adding your favorite nuts, seeds, or dried fruits. You can also adjust the sweetness by using more or less dark chocolate chips or adding a sprinkle of cinnamon. Enjoy this homemade energy-boosting trail mix whenever you need a quick and satisfying snack!

73. Whole Wheat Pretzel Bites

Preparation Time	Cooking Time	Serving Size
20 minutes	10 minutes	Serves 2

INGREDIENTS:

» 1 cup warm water
» 2 1/4 teaspoons active dry yeast
» 1 tablespoon honey or maple syrup
» 2 1/2 cups whole wheat flour
» 1 teaspoon salt
» 2 tablespoons unsalted butter, melted
» Coarse salt, for sprinkling
» 1/4 cup baking soda
» 2 cups boiling water

INSTRUCTIONS:

1. In a small bowl, combine the warm water, active dry yeast, and honey or maple syrup. Stir well and let it sit for about 5 minutes until the mixture becomes frothy.
2. In a large mixing bowl, combine the whole wheat flour and salt. Make a well in the center and pour in the yeast mixture and melted butter.
3. Stir the mixture with a wooden spoon until a dough forms.
4. Transfer the dough onto a lightly floured surface and knead for about 5 minutes until it becomes smooth and elastic.
5. Place the dough in a greased bowl, cover it with a clean kitchen towel, and let it rise in a warm place for about 1 hour or until it doubles in size.
6. Preheat your oven to 425°F (220°C). Line a baking sheet with parchment paper.
7. Punch down the dough to release any air bubbles. Divide it into smaller portions and roll each portion into long ropes about 1/2 inch thick.
8. Cut the ropes into small pieces, about 1 inch in length, to create the pretzel bites.
9. In a shallow bowl, dissolve the baking soda in boiling water.
10. Drop the pretzel bites into the baking soda solution, a few at a time, and let them sit for about 30 seconds. Remove them with a slotted spoon and place them on the prepared baking sheet.
11. Sprinkle the pretzel bites with coarse salt.
12. Bake the pretzel bites in the preheated oven for about 8-10 minutes until they turn golden brown.
13. Remove the pretzel bites from the oven and let them cool slightly before serving.
14. Serve the whole wheat pretzel bites warm, with your favorite dipping sauce if desired.

Nutritional Facts (per serving): Calories: 250; Protein: 9g; Fat: 4g; Carbohydrates: 48g (net); Fiber: 8g.

Tips: Feel free to experiment with different toppings for the pretzel bites, such as sesame seeds or grated Parmesan cheese. Serve them with mustard, cheese dip, or your favorite sauce for a delicious snack!

74. Apple Cinnamon Muffins

Preparation Time	Cooking Time	Serving Size
15 minutes	20 minutes	Makes 12 muffins

INGREDIENTS:

- » 2 cups whole wheat flour
- » 2 teaspoons baking powder
- » 1/2 teaspoon baking soda
- » 1/2 teaspoon salt
- » 1 teaspoon ground cinnamon
- » 1/4 teaspoon ground nutmeg
- » 1/2 cup unsweetened applesauce
- » 1/2 cup maple syrup or honey
- » 1/4 cup coconut oil, melted
- » 2 large eggs
- » 1 teaspoon vanilla extract
- » 1 cup grated apple (about 1 medium-sized apple)
- » 1/2 cup chopped walnuts or pecans (optional)

INSTRUCTIONS:

1. Preheat your oven to 375°F (190°C). Line a muffin tin with paper liners.
2. In a large mixing bowl, whisk together the whole wheat flour, baking powder, baking soda, salt, cinnamon, and nutmeg.
3. In a separate bowl, whisk together the unsweetened applesauce, maple syrup or honey, melted coconut oil, eggs, and vanilla extract.
4. Pour the wet ingredients into the dry ingredients and stir until just combined. Be careful not to overmix.
5. Gently fold in the grated apple and chopped walnuts or pecans, if using.
6. Divide the batter evenly among the prepared muffin cups, filling each about three-fourths full.
7. Bake the muffins in the preheated oven for about 18-20 minutes or until a toothpick inserted into the center comes out clean.
8. Remove the muffins from the oven and let them cool in the muffin tin for a few minutes. Then transfer them to a wire rack to cool completely.
9. Serve the apple cinnamon muffins as a wholesome and flavorful breakfast or snack.

Nutritional Facts (per muffin): Calories: 180; Protein: 4g; Fat: 8g; Carbohydrates: 25g (net); Fiber: 4g.

Tips: Feel free to add a sprinkle of cinnamon sugar on top of the muffins before baking for an extra touch of sweetness. You can also replace the walnuts or pecans with raisins or dried cranberries if desired. Enjoy these moist and aromatic apple cinnamon muffins!

75. Peanut Butter Banana Smoothie

Preparation Time	Serving Size	Ingredients
5 minutes	Serves 2	

- » 2 ripe bananas
- » 2 tablespoons peanut butter (smooth or crunchy)
- » 1 cup almond milk (or your preferred milk)
- » 1 tablespoon honey or maple syrup (optional, for added sweetness)
- » 1/2 teaspoon vanilla extract
- » Ice cubes, as desired

INSTRUCTIONS:

1. Peel the ripe bananas and break them into chunks.
2. Place the banana chunks, peanut butter, almond milk, honey or maple syrup (if using), and vanilla extract in a blender.
3. Blend the ingredients until smooth and creamy.
4. Add ice cubes to the blender, if desired, and blend again until the smoothie reaches your desired consistency.
5. Pour the peanut butter banana smoothie into glasses and serve immediately.

Nutritional Facts (per serving): Calories: 250; Protein: 6g; Fat: 12g; Carbohydrates: 32g (net); Fiber: 4g.

Tips: Feel free to customize the smoothie by adding a handful of spinach or kale for added nutrition. You can also sprinkle some crushed peanuts or a dash of cinnamon on top for extra flavor. Enjoy this creamy and protein-rich peanut butter banana smoothie as a satisfying breakfast or snack!

76. Roasted Chickpea Snack Mix

Preparation Time	**Cooking Time**	**Serving Size**
5 minutes	30 minutes	Serves 2

INGREDIENTS:

» 1 can chickpeas (15 ounces), rinsed and drained
» 1 tablespoon olive oil
» 1 teaspoon paprika
» 1/2 teaspoon garlic powder
» 1/2 teaspoon cumin
» 1/4 teaspoon salt
» 1/4 teaspoon cayenne pepper (adjust to taste)
» 1/4 cup dried cranberries
» 1/4 cup roasted almonds
» 1/4 cup pumpkin seeds

INSTRUCTIONS:

1. Preheat your oven to 400°F (200°C). Line a baking sheet with parchment paper.
2. In a bowl, toss the rinsed and drained chickpeas with olive oil, paprika, garlic powder, cumin, salt, and cayenne pepper. Make sure the chickpeas are evenly coated with the spice mixture.
3. Spread the seasoned chickpeas in a single layer on the prepared baking sheet.
4. Roast the chickpeas in the preheated oven for about 30 minutes, shaking the baking sheet occasionally, until they become crispy and golden brown.
5. Remove the chickpeas from the oven and let them cool for a few minutes.
6. In a separate bowl, combine the dried cranberries, roasted almonds, and pumpkin seeds.
7. Add the roasted chickpeas to the bowl and toss everything together to create a flavorful snack mix.
8. Serve the roasted chickpea snack mix as a crunchy and protein-packed snack.

Nutritional Facts (per serving): Calories: 280; Protein: 12g; Fat: 12g; Carbohydrates: 33g (net); Fiber: 9g.

Tips: Feel free to experiment with different spices and seasonings for the chickpeas, such as chili powder or smoked paprika, to suit your taste preferences. You can also add other dried fruits, nuts, or seeds to the snack mix for variety. Enjoy this savory and satisfying roasted chickpea snack mix!

77. Fruit and Nut Granola Bars

Preparation Time	Cooking Time	Serving Size
15 minutes	20 minutes	Makes about 8 bars

INGREDIENTS:

» 1 1/2 cups rolled oats
» 1/2 cup mixed nuts, chopped (such as almonds, cashews, and walnuts)
» 1/2 cup dried fruits, chopped (such as cranberries, raisins, or apricots)
» 1/4 cup honey or maple syrup
» 1/4 cup almond butter or peanut butter
» 1 teaspoon vanilla extract
» 1/4 teaspoon salt

INSTRUCTIONS:

1. Preheat your oven to 350°F (175°C). Line a baking dish with parchment paper.
2. In a large mixing bowl, combine the rolled oats, chopped mixed nuts, and dried fruits.
3. In a small saucepan, heat the honey or maple syrup, almond butter or peanut butter, vanilla extract, and salt over low heat. Stir until the mixture becomes smooth and well combined.
4. Pour the warm honey or maple syrup mixture over the dry ingredients in the bowl. Mix well until all the ingredients are evenly coated.
5. Transfer the mixture to the lined baking dish. Press it down firmly and evenly to create a compact layer.
6. Bake the granola bars in the preheated oven for about 20 minutes or until the edges turn golden brown.
7. Remove the baking dish from the oven and let it cool completely.
8. Once cooled, cut the granola mixture into bars.
9. Serve the fruit and nut granola bars as a nutritious and on-the-go snack.

Nutritional Facts (per serving, 1 bar): Calories: 200; Protein: 6g; Fat: 9g; Carbohydrates: 26g (net); Fiber: 4g.

Tips: Feel free to add additional ingredients to the granola bars, such as chia seeds, flaxseeds, or shredded coconut. You can also drizzle melted dark chocolate over the top for a touch of indulgence. Store the granola bars in an airtight container for longer shelf life. Enjoy these homemade fruit and nut granola bars as a wholesome and tasty snack!

78. Baked Zucchini Fries with Marinara

Preparation Time	Cooking Time	Serving Size
15 minutes	20 minutes	Serves 2

INGREDIENTS:

- » For the Zucchini Fries:
- » 2 medium zucchini
- » 1/2 cup breadcrumbs (preferably whole wheat)
- » 1/4 cup grated Parmesan cheese
- » 1/2 teaspoon garlic powder
- » 1/2 teaspoon paprika
- » 1/4 teaspoon salt
- » 2 large eggs, beaten
- » Cooking spray
- » For the Marinara Sauce:
- » 1 cup marinara sauce (store-bought or homemade)

INSTRUCTIONS:

1. Preheat your oven to 425°F (220°C). Line a baking sheet with parchment paper and lightly coat it with cooking spray.
2. Cut the zucchini into sticks resembling french fries.
3. In a shallow bowl, combine the breadcrumbs, grated Parmesan cheese, garlic powder, paprika, and salt. Mix well.
4. Dip each zucchini stick into the beaten eggs, ensuring it is fully coated.
5. Roll the egg-coated zucchini stick in the breadcrumb mixture, pressing gently to adhere the breadcrumbs.
6. Place the coated zucchini sticks on the prepared baking sheet in a single layer.
7. Lightly coat the zucchini sticks with cooking spray to help them brown and crisp in the oven.
8. Bake the zucchini fries in the preheated oven for about 15-20 minutes, turning them once halfway through, until they become golden brown and crispy.
9. While the zucchini fries are baking, warm the marinara sauce in a small saucepan over low heat or in the microwave.
10. Serve the baked zucchini fries with the marinara sauce for dipping.

Nutritional Facts (per serving): Calories: 200; Protein: 12g; Fat: 6g; Carbohydrates: 25g (net); Fiber: 4g.

Tips: For a gluten-free version, use gluten-free breadcrumbs or almond flour. You can also add additional spices or herbs to the breadcrumb mixture, such as dried oregano or basil, for extra flavor. Enjoy these crispy and healthier baked zucchini fries with tangy marinara sauce!

79. Oven-Roasted Edamame

Preparation Time	**Cooking Time**	**Serving Size**
5 minutes	15 minutes	Serves 2

INGREDIENTS:

» 2 cups frozen edamame (in pods)
» 1 tablespoon olive oil
» 1/2 teaspoon garlic powder
» 1/4 teaspoon salt
» 1/4 teaspoon black pepper
» Optional toppings: sesame seeds, chili flakes, or grated Parmesan cheese

INSTRUCTIONS:

1. Preheat your oven to 425°F (220°C).
2. In a large bowl, toss the frozen edamame with olive oil, garlic powder, salt, and black pepper until well coated.
3. Spread the seasoned edamame in a single layer on a baking sheet.
4. Roast the edamame in the preheated oven for about 15 minutes, shaking the baking sheet occasionally, until they become slightly crispy and golden.
5. Remove the roasted edamame from the oven and let them cool for a few minutes.
6. Sprinkle the edamame with sesame seeds, chili flakes, or grated Parmesan cheese, if desired.
7. Serve the oven-roasted edamame as a nutritious and protein-rich snack.

Nutritional Facts (per serving): Calories: 150; Protein: 13g; Fat: 7g; Carbohydrates: 9g (net); Fiber: 6g.

Tips: Feel free to experiment with different seasonings for the edamame, such as soy sauce, smoked paprika, or cayenne pepper, to suit your taste preferences. Enjoy these oven-roasted edamame as a tasty and crunchy snack!

80. Dark Chocolate Covered Almonds

Preparation Time	**Cooking Time**	**Chilling Time**
10 minutes	5 minutes	30 minutes

Serving Size: Makes about 1 cup

INGREDIENTS:

» 1 cup whole almonds
» 4 ounces dark chocolate, chopped
» 1/2 teaspoon coconut oil (optional)
» Sea salt, for sprinkling (optional)

INSTRUCTIONS:

1. Line a baking sheet with parchment paper.
2. In a dry skillet over medium heat, toast the almonds, stirring occasionally, for about 5 minutes or until they become fragrant and lightly golden. Remove them from the heat and let them cool completely.
3. In a microwave-safe bowl, combine the dark chocolate and coconut oil, if using. Microwave in 30-second intervals, stirring well between each interval, until the chocolate is melted and smooth.
4. Add the toasted almonds to the melted chocolate. Stir until all the almonds are fully coated with the chocolate.
5. Using a fork or a slotted spoon, remove the chocolate-coated almonds from the bowl, allowing any excess chocolate to drip off.
6. Place the coated almonds on the prepared baking sheet, spacing them apart.
7. Optional: Sprinkle a small amount of sea salt over the chocolate-covered almonds for a sweet and salty flavor contrast.
8. Refrigerate the baking sheet with the almonds for about 30 minutes or until the chocolate sets.
9. Once the chocolate has hardened, transfer the dark chocolate covered almonds to an airtight container or serve them immediately.

Nutritional Facts (per serving, about 1/4 cup): Calories: 160; Protein: 4g; Fat: 13g; Carbohydrates: 11g (net); Fiber: 3g.

Tips: Feel free to use your preferred type of dark chocolate, such as 70% cocoa or higher, for a rich and intense flavor. You can also experiment with different toppings for the chocolate-covered almonds, such as shredded coconut, chopped dried fruits, or a dusting of cocoa powder. Enjoy these indulgent and satisfying dark chocolate covered almonds as a delightful snack or homemade gift!

81. Raspberry Almond Squares

Preparation Time	Cooking Time	Serving Size
15 minutes	25 minutes	Makes 9 squares

INGREDIENTS:

- » 1 cup almond flour
- » 1/4 cup coconut flour
- » 1/4 cup unsweetened shredded coconut
- » 1/4 cup honey or maple syrup
- » 2 tablespoons coconut oil, melted
- » 1 teaspoon vanilla extract
- » 1/4 teaspoon salt
- » 1/2 cup raspberry jam or preserves
- » 1/4 cup sliced almonds

INSTRUCTIONS:

1. Preheat your oven to 350°F (175°C). Line an 8x8-inch baking dish with parchment paper.
2. In a large mixing bowl, combine the almond flour, coconut flour, shredded coconut, honey or maple syrup, melted coconut oil, vanilla extract, and salt. Mix well until the ingredients are fully combined and form a dough-like consistency.
3. Press about two-thirds of the dough mixture evenly into the bottom of the prepared baking dish to create the base layer.
4. Spread the raspberry jam or preserves over the dough layer.
5. Crumble the remaining dough mixture over the raspberry layer.
6. Sprinkle the sliced almonds evenly over the top.
7. Bake in the preheated oven for about 25 minutes or until the edges turn golden brown.
8. Remove the baking dish from the oven and let it cool completely before cutting into squares.
9. Serve the raspberry almond squares as a delectable and slightly sweet treat.

Nutritional Facts (per serving, 1 square): Calories: 180; Protein: 4g; Fat: 13g; Carbohydrates: 14g (net); Fiber: 3g.

Tips: Feel free to use your favorite type of jam or preserves in place of raspberry for variety. You can also add a sprinkle of powdered sugar on top or serve with a dollop of whipped cream or vanilla ice cream, if desired. Enjoy these raspberry almond squares as a delightful snack or dessert!

82. Flourless Chocolate Cake

Preparation Time	Cooking Time	Serving Size
15 minutes	30 minutes	Serves 2

INGREDIENTS:

- » 4 ounces dark chocolate, chopped
- » 1/2 cup unsalted butter, cubed
- » 1/2 cup granulated sugar
- » 2 large eggs
- » 1 teaspoon vanilla extract
- » Pinch of salt
- » Cocoa powder, for dusting (optional)
- » Fresh berries, for garnish (optional)

INSTRUCTIONS:

1. Preheat your oven to 350°F (175°C). Grease a 6-inch round cake pan and line the bottom with parchment paper.
2. In a microwave-safe bowl, melt the dark chocolate and butter together in short intervals, stirring well between each interval, until the mixture is smooth and fully melted. Alternatively, you can melt them in a heatproof bowl set over a pot of simmering water, stirring until melted.
3. In a separate mixing bowl, whisk together the granulated sugar, eggs, vanilla extract, and salt until well combined.
4. Slowly pour the melted chocolate mixture into the sugar and egg mixture, whisking constantly until smooth.
5. Pour the batter into the prepared cake pan, spreading it evenly.
6. Bake in the preheated oven for about 25-30 minutes or until a toothpick inserted into the center comes out with moist crumbs.
7. Remove the cake from the oven and let it cool in the pan for a few minutes. Then transfer it to a wire rack to cool completely.
8. Optional: Dust the top of the cooled cake with cocoa powder and garnish with fresh berries for a touch of elegance.
9. Slice the flourless chocolate cake and serve it as a rich and decadent dessert.

Nutritional Facts (per serving): Calories: 400; Protein: 6g; Fat: 30g; Carbohydrates: 30g (net); Fiber: 4g.

Tips: For added richness, you can serve the flourless chocolate cake with a scoop of vanilla ice cream or a dollop of whipped cream. The cake can also be stored in an airtight container at room temperature for a few days. Enjoy this indulgent and gluten-free flourless chocolate cake as a special treat!

83. Lemon Cheesecake Bites

Preparation Time	**Chilling Time**	**Serving Size**
15 minutes	2 hours	Makes 12 bites

INGREDIENTS:

» For the Crust:
» 1 cup almond flour
» 2 tablespoons melted coconut oil
» 1 tablespoon honey or maple syrup
» For the Filling:
» 8 ounces cream cheese, softened
» 1/4 cup powdered sweetener (such as erythritol or stevia)
» 2 tablespoons fresh lemon juice
» 1 teaspoon lemon zest
» 1/2 teaspoon vanilla extract

INSTRUCTIONS:

1. In a mixing bowl, combine the almond flour, melted coconut oil, and honey or maple syrup. Stir until the mixture resembles a crumbly texture.
2. Line a mini muffin pan with paper liners.
3. Divide the crust mixture evenly among the muffin cups. Press down firmly to create a compact crust layer.
4. In a separate mixing bowl, beat the softened cream cheese, powdered sweetener, lemon juice, lemon zest, and vanilla extract until smooth and well combined.
5. Spoon the cream cheese mixture over the crust in each muffin cup, filling them almost to the top.
6. Smooth the tops with a spatula or the back of a spoon.
7. Place the muffin pan in the refrigerator and chill the cheesecake bites for at least 2 hours or until firm.
8. Once chilled, remove the paper liners from the cheesecake bites.
9. Serve the lemon cheesecake bites chilled and garnish with additional lemon zest, if desired.

Nutritional Facts (per serving, 1 bite): Calories: 130; Protein: 3g; Fat: 12g; Carbohydrates: 4g (net); Fiber: 1g.

Tips: For a gluten-free option, ensure that the almond flour is certified gluten-free. You can also add a small dollop of sugar-free whipped cream on top of each bite for added decadence. Enjoy these creamy and tangy lemon cheesecake bites as a delightful dessert or snack!

84. Keto Peanut Butter Cookies

Preparation Time	Cooking Time	Serving Size
10 minutes	12 minutes	Makes about 12 cookies

INGREDIENTS:

» 1 cup natural peanut butter (unsweetened, no added oils)

» 1/2 cup powdered sweetener (such as erythritol or stevia)

» 1 large egg

» 1/2 teaspoon vanilla extract

» Optional: 1/4 cup sugar-free chocolate chips

INSTRUCTIONS:

1. Preheat your oven to 350°F (175°C). Line a baking sheet with parchment paper.
2. In a mixing bowl, combine the natural peanut butter, powdered sweetener, egg, and vanilla extract. Mix well until all the ingredients are fully incorporated and form a cookie dough-like consistency.
3. Optional: Fold in the sugar-free chocolate chips into the cookie dough for added flavor and texture.
4. Roll the cookie dough into small balls, about 1 tablespoon each.
5. Place the cookie dough balls on the prepared baking sheet, spacing them apart. Use a fork to gently flatten each ball in a crisscross pattern.
6. Bake in the preheated oven for about 10-12 minutes or until the cookies turn golden brown around the edges.
7. Remove the baking sheet from the oven and let the cookies cool on the sheet for a few minutes. Then transfer them to a wire rack to cool completely.
8. Serve the keto peanut butter cookies as a delicious and low-carb treat.

Nutritional Facts (per serving, 1 cookie): Calories: 130; Protein: 5g; Fat: 11g; Carbohydrates: 4g (net); Fiber: 1g.

Tips: Make sure to use natural peanut butter without added oils or sugar for a keto-friendly option. You can also substitute the peanut butter with almond butter or other nut butter of your choice. Enjoy these keto peanut butter cookies as a guilt-free and satisfying snack!

85. Low Carb Strawberry Shortcake

Preparation Time	Cooking Time	Chilling Time
20 minutes	20 minutes	30 minutes

Serving Size: Serves 2

INGREDIENTS:

- » For the Shortcakes:
- » 1 cup almond flour
- » 2 tablespoons coconut flour
- » 2 tablespoons powdered sweetener (such as erythritol or stevia)
- » 1 teaspoon baking powder
- » 1/4 teaspoon salt
- » 2 tablespoons unsalted butter, cold and cubed
- » 1/4 cup heavy cream
- » 1/2 teaspoon vanilla extract
- » For the Strawberry Filling:
- » 1 cup fresh strawberries, sliced
- » 1 tablespoon powdered sweetener (such as erythritol or stevia)
- » Whipped cream, for topping (optional)

INSTRUCTIONS:

1. Preheat your oven to 350°F (175°C). Line a baking sheet with parchment paper.
2. In a mixing bowl, whisk together the almond flour, coconut flour, powdered sweetener, baking powder, and salt.
3. Add the cold and cubed unsalted butter to the dry ingredients. Use a pastry cutter or your fingers to cut the butter into the flour mixture until it resembles coarse crumbs.
4. Pour in the heavy cream and vanilla extract. Stir until the dough comes together. It should be slightly sticky but manageable.
5. Transfer the dough onto a lightly floured surface. Gently knead it a few times to ensure it holds together.
6. Roll out the dough to about 1/2-inch thickness. Use a biscuit cutter or a glass to cut out shortcakes. Place them on the prepared baking sheet.
7. Bake in the preheated oven for about 18-20 minutes or until the shortcakes turn golden brown.
8. Remove the baking sheet from the oven and let the shortcakes cool completely on a wire rack.
9. In a bowl, combine the sliced strawberries and powdered sweetener. Toss gently to coat the strawberries.
10. Slice the cooled shortcakes horizontally. Place a spoonful of the strawberry filling on the bottom half of each shortcake. Top with whipped cream, if desired. Place the top half of the shortcake on the filling.
11. Serve the low-carb strawberry shortcakes as a delightful and guilt-free dessert.

Nutritional Facts (per serving): Calories: 300; Protein: 8g; Fat: 26g; Carbohydrates: 11g (net); Fiber: 5g.

Tips: Feel free to substitute the strawberries with other low-carb berries, such as raspberries or blueberries. You can also add a dollop of sugar-free whipped cream on top for extra indulgence. Enjoy this low-carb version of strawberry shortcake as a satisfying and keto-friendly dessert!

86. Dark Chocolate Avocado Mousse

Preparation Time	Chilling Time	Serving Size
10 minutes	1 hour	Serves 2

INGREDIENTS:

- » 1 ripe avocado
- » 3 tablespoons unsweetened cocoa powder
- » 2 tablespoons honey or maple syrup
- » 1/4 cup unsweetened almond milk (or your preferred milk)
- » 1/2 teaspoon vanilla extract
- » Pinch of salt
- » Optional toppings: dark chocolate shavings, sliced almonds, or fresh berries

INSTRUCTIONS:

1. Cut the avocado in half and remove the pit. Scoop out the flesh and place it in a blender or food processor.
2. Add the cocoa powder, honey or maple syrup, almond milk, vanilla extract, and salt to the blender or food processor.
3. Blend or process the ingredients until smooth and creamy, scraping down the sides as needed.
4. Divide the dark chocolate avocado mousse into serving glasses or bowls.
5. Optional: Top with dark chocolate shavings, sliced almonds, or fresh berries for added texture and flavor.
6. Refrigerate the mousse for at least 1 hour to chill and set.
7. Serve the chilled dark chocolate avocado mousse as a rich and indulgent dessert.

Nutritional Facts (per serving): Calories: 200; Protein: 4g; Fat: 16g; Carbohydrates: 17g (net); Fiber: 8g.

Tips: For a sweeter mousse, you can add more honey or maple syrup to taste. Feel free to adjust the cocoa powder amount to suit your preference for a more intense chocolate flavor. Enjoy this creamy and healthier dark chocolate avocado mousse as a guilt-free dessert!

87. Cinnamon Almond Protein Bars

Preparation Time	Chilling Time	Serving Size
15 minutes	1 hour	Makes 6 bars

INGREDIENTS:

- » 1 cup almond butter
- » 1/4 cup honey or maple syrup
- » 1/2 cup vanilla protein powder
- » 1/2 cup almond flour
- » 1 teaspoon cinnamon
- » 1/4 teaspoon salt
- » 1/4 cup unsweetened almond milk (or your preferred milk)
- » Optional: 1/4 cup chopped almonds or other nuts for added crunch

INSTRUCTIONS:

1. In a mixing bowl, combine the almond butter and honey or maple syrup. Stir until well mixed.
2. Add the vanilla protein powder, almond flour, cinnamon, and salt to the bowl. Mix until all the ingredients are evenly incorporated.
3. Slowly pour in the almond milk, a little at a time, until the mixture comes together and forms a thick dough.
4. Optional: Fold in the chopped almonds or other nuts to add crunch and texture to the bars.
5. Line an 8x8-inch baking dish with parchment paper.
6. Press the mixture firmly and evenly into the lined baking dish to create a compact layer.
7. Refrigerate the baking dish for at least 1 hour or until the bars are firm.
8. Once chilled, remove the protein bars from the baking dish and cut them into 6 equal-sized bars.
9. Serve the cinnamon almond protein bars as a nutritious and energizing snack.

Nutritional Facts (per serving, 1 bar): Calories: 280; Protein: 15g; Fat: 20g; Carbohydrates: 14g (net); Fiber: 4g.

Tips: Feel free to customize the protein bars by adding other ingredients such as chia seeds, flaxseeds, or dried fruits. You can also drizzle melted dark chocolate on top for an extra touch of indulgence. Store the bars in an airtight container in the refrigerator for longer shelf life. Enjoy these cinnamon almond protein bars as a healthy and satisfying snack!

88. Coconut Cream Pie

Preparation Time	Chilling Time	Serving Size
30 minutes	2 hours	Serves 2

INGREDIENTS:

- » For the Crust:
- » 1 cup almond flour
- » 2 tablespoons coconut flour
- » 2 tablespoons melted coconut oil
- » 1 tablespoon honey or maple syrup
- » For the Filling:
- » 1 can full-fat coconut milk (13.5 ounces)
- » 1/4 cup honey or maple syrup
- » 2 tablespoons cornstarch or arrowroot powder
- » 1/4 teaspoon salt
- » 1/2 teaspoon vanilla extract
- » For the Topping:
- » 1 cup whipped coconut cream (from refrigerated full-fat coconut milk)
- » Toasted coconut flakes, for garnish

INSTRUCTIONS:

1. In a mixing bowl, combine the almond flour, coconut flour, melted coconut oil, and honey or maple syrup. Stir until the mixture resembles a crumbly texture.
2. Press the crust mixture into the bottom of two individual serving dishes or a small pie dish. Press down firmly to create an even crust layer.
3. Place the crust in the refrigerator to chill while preparing the filling.
4. In a saucepan, combine the coconut milk, honey or maple syrup, cornstarch or arrowroot powder, and salt. Whisk until well combined.
5. Heat the saucepan over medium heat, stirring constantly, until the mixture thickens and comes to a gentle boil.
6. Remove the saucepan from the heat and stir in the vanilla extract.
7. Pour the coconut cream filling over the chilled crust in the serving dishes or pie dish.
8. Place the coconut cream pie in the refrigerator to chill for at least 2 hours or until the filling sets.
9. Once chilled and set, remove the coconut cream pie from the refrigerator.
10. Top the pie with whipped coconut cream and garnish with toasted coconut flakes.
11. Serve the coconut cream pie as a luscious and tropical dessert.

Nutritional Facts (per serving): Calories: 400; Protein: 4g; Fat: 32g; Carbohydrates: 25g (net); Fiber: 4g.

Tips: For an extra touch of flavor, you can add a teaspoon of coconut extract to the filling. Feel free to customize the pie by adding a layer of sliced bananas or fresh berries between the crust and filling. Enjoy this creamy and dreamy coconut cream pie as a delightful dessert!

89. Blueberry Lemon Ricotta Pancakes

Preparation Time	Cooking Time	Serving Size
10 minutes	15 minutes	Makes about 8 pancakes

INGREDIENTS:

» 1 cup all-purpose flour
» 2 tablespoons granulated sugar
» 1 teaspoon baking powder
» 1/2 teaspoon baking soda
» 1/4 teaspoon salt
» 3/4 cup ricotta cheese
» 1/2 cup milk
» 1 large egg
» 1 tablespoon melted butter
» 1 teaspoon vanilla extract
» Zest of 1 lemon
» 1 cup fresh blueberries

INSTRUCTIONS:

1. In a mixing bowl, whisk together the flour, sugar, baking powder, baking soda, and salt.
2. In a separate bowl, combine the ricotta cheese, milk, egg, melted butter, vanilla extract, and lemon zest. Mix until well blended.
3. Pour the wet ingredients into the bowl with the dry ingredients. Stir until just combined. Do not overmix; it's okay if the batter is slightly lumpy.
4. Gently fold in the fresh blueberries into the pancake batter.
5. Preheat a non-stick skillet or griddle over medium heat. Lightly grease the cooking surface with butter or cooking spray.
6. Using a 1/4-cup measuring cup, pour the pancake batter onto the hot skillet. Cook until bubbles form on the surface, then flip the pancake and cook for another 1-2 minutes, or until golden brown.
7. Repeat the process with the remaining batter, adding more butter or cooking spray to the skillet as needed.
8. Serve the blueberry lemon ricotta pancakes warm with your favorite toppings, such as maple syrup, additional blueberries, or a dusting of powdered sugar.

Nutritional Facts (per serving, 2 pancakes): Calories: 250; Protein: 10g; Fat: 8g; Carbohydrates: 35g; Fiber: 2g.

Tips: For extra lemon flavor, you can add a squeeze of fresh lemon juice to the pancake batter. If you prefer a lighter texture, you can separate the egg and whip the egg white until stiff peaks form. Fold in the whipped egg white at the end to make the pancakes fluffier. Feel free to substitute fresh blueberries with other fruits, such as raspberries or sliced strawberries, to suit your preference.

Enjoy these delightful blueberry lemon ricotta pancakes as a delicious breakfast or brunch treat!

90. Chocolate Almond Butter Fudge

Preparation Time	Chilling Time	Serving Size
10 minutes	2 hours	Makes about 16 squares

INGREDIENTS:

- » 1 cup almond butter
- » 1/4 cup coconut oil
- » 1/4 cup unsweetened cocoa powder
- » 1/4 cup powdered sweetener (such as erythritol or stevia)
- » 1 teaspoon vanilla extract
- » Pinch of salt
- » Optional toppings: crushed almonds, sea salt flakes, or cocoa powder

INSTRUCTIONS:

1. In a microwave-safe bowl or small saucepan, melt the almond butter and coconut oil together until smooth and well combined.
2. Stir in the cocoa powder, powdered sweetener, vanilla extract, and salt until the mixture is smooth and free of lumps.
3. Pour the chocolate almond butter mixture into a parchment-lined square baking dish. Smooth the top with a spatula.
4. Optional: Sprinkle crushed almonds, sea salt flakes, or a dusting of cocoa powder on top for added flavor and texture.
5. Place the baking dish in the refrigerator and chill the fudge for at least 2 hours, or until firm.
6. Once chilled and set, remove the fudge from the baking dish and cut it into small squares.
7. Serve the chocolate almond butter fudge as a rich and decadent treat.

Nutritional Facts (per serving, 1 square): Calories: 120; Protein: 3g; Fat: 11g; Carbohydrates: 4g; Fiber: 2g.

Tips: Feel free to use other nut or seed butters in place of almond butter, such as peanut butter or sunflower seed butter. Adjust the sweetness level by adding more or less powdered sweetener according to your taste preference. Store the fudge in an airtight container in the refrigerator for longer shelf life.

Enjoy this creamy and satisfying chocolate almond butter fudge as a delightful and guilt-free treat!

91. Banana Bread Pudding

Preparation Time	Cooking Time	Chilling Time
15 minutes	40 minutes	1 hour

Serving Size: Serves 2

INGREDIENTS:

- » 2 ripe bananas, mashed
- » 1 cup milk (dairy or plant-based)
- » 2 large eggs
- » 1/4 cup granulated sugar
- » 1 teaspoon vanilla extract
- » 4 cups stale bread, cubed (such as French bread or brioche)
- » 1/4 cup dark chocolate chips
- » Optional toppings: powdered sugar, sliced bananas, or whipped cream

INSTRUCTIONS:

1. Preheat your oven to 350°F (175°C). Grease a small baking dish.
2. In a mixing bowl, whisk together the mashed bananas, milk, eggs, granulated sugar, and vanilla extract until well combined.
3. Add the cubed stale bread to the banana mixture and gently toss to coat all the bread pieces. Let the bread soak in the mixture for about 10 minutes.
4. Fold in the dark chocolate chips into the bread mixture, ensuring they are evenly distributed.
5. Transfer the bread mixture to the greased baking dish and spread it out evenly.
6. Bake in the preheated oven for about 40 minutes or until the top is golden brown and the pudding is set.
7. Remove the baking dish from the oven and let the bread pudding cool for a few minutes.
8. Once cooled, refrigerate the bread pudding for at least 1 hour to chill and set.
9. Serve the chilled banana bread pudding with optional toppings such as a dusting of powdered sugar, sliced bananas, or a dollop of whipped cream.

Nutritional Facts (per serving): Calories: 350; Protein: 10g; Fat: 10g; Carbohydrates: 55g; Fiber: 4g.

Tips: For a twist, you can add a sprinkle of cinnamon or a dash of nutmeg to the banana mixture for extra flavor.; If you don't have stale bread, you can toast fresh bread cubes in the oven for a few minutes until slightly dry before using them in the recipe.; Feel free to customize the bread pudding by adding chopped nuts or dried fruits to the mixture for added texture and taste.; Enjoy this comforting and delicious banana bread pudding as a delightful dessert or even a special breakfast treat!

92. Dark Chocolate Chip Oat Cookies.

Preparation Time	Cooking Time	Serving Size
15 minutes	12 minutes	Makes about 12 cookies

INGREDIENTS:

» 1 cup rolled oats
» 1/2 cup whole wheat flour
» 1/4 cup coconut oil, melted
» 1/4 cup honey or maple syrup
» 1 large egg
» 1/2 teaspoon vanilla extract
» 1/4 teaspoon baking soda
» Pinch of salt
» 1/4 cup dark chocolate chips
» Optional: 1/4 cup chopped nuts (such as almonds or walnuts)

INSTRUCTIONS:

1. Preheat your oven to 350°F (175°C). Line a baking sheet with parchment paper.
2. In a mixing bowl, combine the rolled oats, whole wheat flour, melted coconut oil, honey or maple syrup, egg, vanilla extract, baking soda, and salt. Mix until all the ingredients are well incorporated.
3. Fold in the dark chocolate chips (and chopped nuts if using) into the cookie dough, ensuring they are evenly distributed.
4. Using a tablespoon or cookie scoop, drop the cookie dough onto the lined baking sheet, spacing them apart.
5. Gently flatten each cookie dough mound with the back of a spoon or your fingers to create a round shape.
6. Bake in the preheated oven for about 10-12 minutes or until the edges turn golden brown.
7. Remove the baking sheet from the oven and let the cookies cool on the sheet for a few minutes. Then transfer them to a wire rack to cool completely.
8. Once cooled, serve the dark chocolate chip oat cookies as a wholesome and tasty snack.

Nutritional Facts (per serving, 1 cookie): Calories: 120; Protein: 3g; Fat: 6g; Carbohydrates: 15g; Fiber: 2g.

Tips: Feel free to experiment with different types of chocolate, such as semi-sweet or milk chocolate, depending on your preference.

- You can also add other mix-ins to the cookies, such as dried fruits or shredded coconut, for added variety and texture.
- Store the cookies in an airtight container at room temperature for a few days.

Enjoy these delightful and healthier dark chocolate chip oat cookies as a guilt-free treat!

93. Apple Cinnamon Oatmeal Bars

Preparation Time	Cooking Time	Serving Size
15 minutes	35 minutes	Makes about 12 bars

INGREDIENTS:

- » 2 cups old-fashioned oats
- » 1 cup whole wheat flour
- » 1/2 cup coconut oil, melted
- » 1/2 cup honey or maple syrup
- » 1 teaspoon cinnamon
- » 1/2 teaspoon baking soda
- » 1/4 teaspoon salt
- » 2 medium apples, peeled and diced
- » 1/4 cup chopped walnuts (optional)

INSTRUCTIONS:

1. Preheat your oven to 350°F (175°C). Grease or line a square baking dish.
2. In a mixing bowl, combine the oats, whole wheat flour, melted coconut oil, honey or maple syrup, cinnamon, baking soda, and salt. Mix until all the ingredients are well combined.
3. Reserve 1/2 cup of the oat mixture for the topping.
4. Press the remaining oat mixture firmly into the bottom of the prepared baking dish to create an even layer.
5. Evenly distribute the diced apples over the oat layer.
6. Optional: Sprinkle the chopped walnuts on top of the apples for added crunch and flavor.
7. Crumble the reserved oat mixture over the apples to create the topping.
8. Bake in the preheated oven for about 30-35 minutes or until the top turns golden brown and the apples are tender.
9. Remove the baking dish from the oven and let the bars cool completely before cutting into squares.
10. Serve the apple cinnamon oatmeal bars as a delicious and wholesome snack or dessert.

Nutritional Facts (per serving, 1 bar): Calories: 220; Protein: 4g; Fat: 10g; Carbohydrates: 30g; Fiber: 4g.

Tips: Feel free to add other spices such as nutmeg or cloves to the oat mixture for additional warmth and flavor.

- You can use a mix of apple varieties for a more complex flavor profile.
- Store the oatmeal bars in an airtight container at room temperature for a few days, or refrigerate them for longer shelf life.

Enjoy these apple cinnamon oatmeal bars as a delicious and nutritious treat!

94. Mixed Berry Cobbler

Preparation Time	Cooking Time	Serving Size
15 minutes	35 minutes	Serves 2

INGREDIENTS:

» 2 cups mixed berries (such as blueberries, raspberries, and strawberries)
» 1 tablespoon lemon juice
» 2 tablespoons granulated sugar
» 1 tablespoon cornstarch
» 1/2 cup all-purpose flour
» 2 tablespoons granulated sugar
» 1/2 teaspoon baking powder
» 1/4 teaspoon salt
» 3 tablespoons cold unsalted butter, cubed
» 1/4 cup milk (dairy or plant-based)

INSTRUCTIONS:

1. Preheat your oven to 375°F (190°C). Grease a small baking dish.
2. In a bowl, combine the mixed berries, lemon juice, granulated sugar, and cornstarch. Toss gently until the berries are coated.
3. Transfer the berry mixture to the greased baking dish and spread it out evenly.
4. In a separate bowl, whisk together the flour, granulated sugar, baking powder, and salt.
5. Add the cold cubed butter to the flour mixture. Use a pastry cutter or your fingers to cut the butter into the flour until it resembles coarse crumbs.
6. Pour in the milk and stir until the mixture comes together to form a dough-like consistency.
7. Drop spoonfuls of the dough over the berry mixture, covering as much of the surface as possible.
8. Bake in the preheated oven for about 30-35 minutes or until the topping turns golden brown and the berries are bubbling.
9. Remove the baking dish from the oven and let the cobbler cool for a few minutes before serving.
10. Serve the mixed berry cobbler warm as a delightful and fruity dessert. Optional: Top with a scoop of vanilla ice cream or whipped cream.

Nutritional Facts (per serving): Calories: 300; Protein: 4g; Fat: 12g; Carbohydrates: 47g; Fiber: 5g.

Tips: Feel free to use any combination of your favorite berries or use frozen berries if fresh ones are not available.

- You can adjust the sweetness level by adding more or less sugar, depending on the natural sweetness of the berries.
- Enjoy the cobbler on its own or pair it with your preferred toppings, such as ice cream or yogurt.

95. Chocolate-Dipped Strawberries

Preparation Time	Chilling Time	Serving Size
15 minutes	30 minutes	Makes about 12 strawberries

INGREDIENTS:

» 12 fresh strawberries, stems intact
» 4 ounces dark chocolate, chopped
» Optional toppings: chopped nuts, shredded coconut, or sprinkles

INSTRUCTIONS:

1. Line a baking sheet with parchment paper.
2. In a heatproof bowl, melt the chopped dark chocolate using a microwave or a double boiler. Stir occasionally until smooth and fully melted.
3. Hold a strawberry by the stem and dip it into the melted chocolate, swirling it to coat the bottom two-thirds of the strawberry.
4. Lift the strawberry out of the chocolate and let the excess chocolate drip off.
5. Optional: While the chocolate is still wet, roll the dipped strawberry in your preferred topping, such as chopped nuts, shredded coconut, or sprinkles.
6. Place the chocolate-dipped strawberry on the lined baking sheet.
7. Repeat the process with the remaining strawberries.
8. Once all the strawberries are dipped and decorated, place the baking sheet in the refrigerator for about 30 minutes to allow the chocolate to set.
9. Once the chocolate is firm, remove the strawberries from the refrigerator and serve them as a delightful and elegant dessert.

Nutritional Facts (per serving, 1 strawberry): Calories: 50; Protein: 1g; Fat: 3g; Carbohydrates: 7g; Fiber: 1g.

Tips: Use ripe and firm strawberries for the best results.

- Feel free to use milk or white chocolate instead of dark chocolate if preferred.
- You can drizzle additional melted chocolate over the dipped strawberries for a decorative touch.

Enjoy these chocolate-dipped strawberries as a delicious and romantic treat!

96. Almond Joy Energy Balls

Preparation Time	Chilling Time	Serving Size
15 minutes	30 minutes	Makes about 12 energy balls

INGREDIENTS:

» 1 cup pitted dates
» 1 cup unsweetened shredded coconut
» 1/2 cup raw almonds
» 2 tablespoons unsweetened cocoa powder
» 2 tablespoons almond butter
» 1 tablespoon honey or maple syrup
» 1/2 teaspoon vanilla extract
» Pinch of salt
» Optional: 1/4 cup dark chocolate chips, chopped almonds, or shredded coconut for rolling

INSTRUCTIONS:

1. In a food processor, blend the pitted dates, shredded coconut, raw almonds, cocoa powder, almond butter, honey or maple syrup, vanilla extract, and salt until the mixture comes together and forms a sticky dough.
2. Optional: Add the dark chocolate chips, chopped almonds, or shredded coconut to the mixture and pulse a few times to incorporate.
3. Scoop out about a tablespoon of the mixture and roll it between your palms to form a ball. Repeat with the remaining mixture.
4. Optional: Roll the energy balls in chopped almonds, shredded coconut, or dark chocolate chips for extra flavor and texture.
5. Place the energy balls on a parchment-lined baking sheet and refrigerate for about 30 minutes to firm up.
6. Once chilled and firm, store the almond joy energy balls in an airtight container in the refrigerator for up to 2 weeks.
7. Enjoy the almond joy energy balls as a quick and nutritious snack.

Nutritional Facts (per serving, 1 energy ball): Calories: 100; Protein: 2g; Fat: 7g; Carbohydrates: 10g; Fiber: 2g.

Tips: Make sure the dates are soft and pliable. If they're dry, soak them in warm water for a few minutes before blending.

- Feel free to customize the energy balls by adding other ingredients such as chia seeds, flaxseeds, or dried fruits.
- Adjust the sweetness level by adding more or less honey or maple syrup according to your taste preference.

Enjoy these homemade almond joy energy balls as a healthy and satisfying snack!

97. Baked Apples with Cinnamon

Preparation Time	Baking Time	Serving Size
10 minutes	30 minutes	Serves 2

INGREDIENTS:

» 2 apples (such as Granny Smith or Honeycrisp)
» 2 tablespoons unsalted butter or coconut oil, melted
» 2 tablespoons honey or maple syrup
» 1 teaspoon ground cinnamon
» Optional toppings: chopped nuts, raisins, or a dollop of yogurt

INSTRUCTIONS:

1. Preheat your oven to 375°F (190°C). Grease a baking dish or line it with parchment paper.
2. Cut the apples in half horizontally and remove the cores and seeds. Place the apple halves in the prepared baking dish.
3. In a small bowl, whisk together the melted butter or coconut oil, honey or maple syrup, and ground cinnamon until well combined.
4. Drizzle the cinnamon mixture evenly over the apple halves, making sure to coat the entire surface.
5. Place the baking dish in the preheated oven and bake for about 25-30 minutes or until the apples are tender and golden.
6. Remove the baked apples from the oven and let them cool slightly.
7. Serve the baked apples warm as a comforting and nutritious dessert.
8. Optional: Top the baked apples with chopped nuts, raisins, or a dollop of yogurt for added flavor and texture.

Nutritional Facts (per serving): Calories: 150; Protein: 1g; Fat: 7g; Carbohydrates: 25g; Fiber: 4g.

Tips:

- You can use any variety of apples that you prefer, depending on your taste and texture preferences.
- Feel free to adjust the sweetness level by adding more or less honey or maple syrup, according to the natural sweetness of the apples.
- Experiment with different spice combinations, such as adding a pinch of nutmeg or cloves, for a unique flavor twist.
- Enjoy these baked apples with cinnamon as a simple and delicious dessert or even a cozy breakfast treat!

98. Pumpkin Spice Donuts.

Preparation Time	Baking Time	Serving Size
15 minutes	15 minutes	Makes about 12 donuts

INGREDIENTS:

» For the Donuts:
» 1 3/4 cups all-purpose flour
» 1/2 cup granulated sugar
» 1 1/2 teaspoons baking powder
» 1/2 teaspoon baking soda
» 1/2 teaspoon ground cinnamon
» 1/4 teaspoon ground nutmeg
» 1/4 teaspoon ground ginger
» 1/4 teaspoon salt
» 3/4 cup pumpkin puree
» 1/2 cup milk (dairy or plant-based)
» 1/4 cup melted unsalted butter or coconut oil
» 1 large egg
» 1 teaspoon vanilla extract
» For the Glaze:
» 1 cup powdered sugar
» 2 tablespoons milk (dairy or plant-based)
» 1/2 teaspoon vanilla extract
» Optional: Ground cinnamon for dusting

INSTRUCTIONS:

1. Preheat your oven to 350°F (175°C). Grease a donut pan.
2. In a large bowl, whisk together the flour, sugar, baking powder, baking soda, ground cinnamon, ground nutmeg, ground ginger, and salt.
3. In a separate bowl, whisk together the pumpkin puree, milk, melted butter or coconut oil, egg, and vanilla extract until well combined.
4. Pour the wet ingredients into the bowl with the dry ingredients. Stir until just combined. Do not overmix; it's okay if there are a few lumps.
5. Spoon the batter into a piping bag or a zip-top bag with one corner snipped off.
6. Pipe the batter into the prepared donut pan, filling each cavity about two-thirds full.
7. Bake in the preheated oven for about 12-15 minutes or until a toothpick inserted into a donut comes out clean.
8. Remove the donuts from the oven and let them cool in the pan for a few minutes before transferring them to a wire rack to cool completely.
9. In a small bowl, whisk together the powdered sugar, milk, and vanilla extract until a smooth glaze forms.
10. Dip each cooled donut into the glaze, allowing any excess to drip off. Place the glazed donuts back on the wire rack.
11. Optional: Dust the glazed donuts with ground cinnamon for an extra touch of flavor.
12. Let the glaze set for a few minutes before serving the pumpkin spice donuts.

Nutritional Facts (per serving, 1 donut): Calories: 180; Protein: 2g; Fat: 5g; Carbohydrates: 31g; Fiber: 1g.

Tips: If you don't have a donut pan, you can use a muffin pan and create donut-shaped holes by using a small biscuit cutter or the end of a round piping tip.

- For an extra boost of flavor, you can add a pinch of cloves or allspice to the spice mixture.
- Store the glazed donuts in an airtight container at room temperature for a few days.

Enjoy these pumpkin spice donuts as a delightful fall treat, perfect for breakfast or a cozy dessert!

99. Chewy Maple Oat Clusters

Preparation Time	Baking Time	Serving Size
10 minutes	25 minutes	Makes about 12 clusters

INGREDIENTS:

- » 2 cups old-fashioned oats
- » 1/2 cup chopped nuts (such as almonds or walnuts)
- » 1/4 cup maple syrup
- » 1/4 cup coconut oil, melted
- » 1/4 cup packed brown sugar
- » 1/2 teaspoon vanilla extract
- » Pinch of salt

INSTRUCTIONS:

1. Preheat your oven to 325°F (160°C). Line a baking sheet with parchment paper.
2. In a large bowl, combine the oats and chopped nuts.
3. In a separate bowl, whisk together the maple syrup, melted coconut oil, brown sugar, vanilla extract, and salt until well blended.
4. Pour the maple syrup mixture over the oat and nut mixture. Stir until all the oats and nuts are coated with the mixture.
5. Drop spoonfuls of the mixture onto the prepared baking sheet, forming clusters. Press them gently to ensure they hold their shape.
6. Bake in the preheated oven for about 25 minutes or until the clusters turn golden brown.
7. Remove the baking sheet from the oven and let the clusters cool completely on the sheet.
8. Once cooled, carefully lift the clusters off the parchment paper and store them in an airtight container.
9. Enjoy the chewy maple oat clusters as a delicious and wholesome snack.

Nutritional Facts (per serving, 1 cluster): Calories: 150; Protein: 3g; Fat: 9g; Carbohydrates: 16g; Fiber: 2g.

Tips: Feel free to add other mix-ins to the clusters, such as dried fruits, coconut flakes, or chocolate chips, for added variety and texture.

- You can customize the sweetness by adjusting the amount of maple syrup or brown sugar according to your taste preference.

Enjoy these homemade chewy maple oat clusters as a satisfying and nutritious snack!

100. Vegan Chocolate Brownies

Preparation Time	**Baking Time**	**Serving Size**
15 minutes	25 minutes	Makes about 12 brownies

INGREDIENTS:

» 1 cup all-purpose flour
» 1/2 cup unsweetened cocoa powder
» 1/2 teaspoon baking powder
» 1/4 teaspoon baking soda
» 1/4 teaspoon salt
» 1/2 cup coconut oil, melted
» 1/2 cup unsweetened applesauce
» 3/4 cup granulated sugar
» 1/4 cup maple syrup or agave nectar
» 1 teaspoon vanilla extract
» 1/2 cup vegan chocolate chips

INSTRUCTIONS:

1. Preheat your oven to 350°F (175°C). Grease or line a square baking dish.
2. In a mixing bowl, whisk together the flour, cocoa powder, baking powder, baking soda, and salt.
3. In a separate bowl, whisk together the melted coconut oil, applesauce, granulated sugar, maple syrup or agave nectar, and vanilla extract until well combined.
4. Pour the wet ingredients into the bowl with the dry ingredients. Stir until just combined. Do not overmix; it's okay if there are a few lumps.
5. Fold in the vegan chocolate chips into the batter, ensuring they are evenly distributed.
6. Pour the batter into the prepared baking dish and spread it out evenly.
7. Bake in the preheated oven for about 25 minutes or until a toothpick inserted into the center comes out with a few moist crumbs.
8. Remove the baking dish from the oven and let the brownies cool completely before cutting into squares.
9. Enjoy the vegan chocolate brownies as a decadent and indulgent treat.

Nutritional Facts (per serving, 1 brownie): Calories: 180; Protein: 2g; Fat: 9g; Carbohydrates: 24g; Fiber: 2g.

Tips: Feel free to add chopped nuts or swirl in some peanut butter or almond butter into the batter for additional flavor and texture.

- You can use other sweeteners such as coconut sugar or date syrup as a substitute for granulated sugar.
- Store the brownies in an airtight container at room temperature for a few days.

Enjoy these vegan chocolate brownies as a delicious and cruelty-free dessert!

CHAPTER 7
Meal Plans and Practical Advice

High Carb Meal Plan

Day 1

Breakfast: Banana and Blueberry Pancakes
Lunch: Lentil and Sweet Potato Salad
Dinner: Vegan Chickpea Curry with Brown Rice

Snacks: Baked Sweet Potato Fries
Dessert: Banana Bread Pudding

Day 2

Breakfast: Oats and Apple Porridge
Lunch: Chickpea Avocado Toast
Dinner: Loaded Veggie Pizza

Snacks: Energy-Boosting Trail Mix
Dessert: Dark Chocolate Chip Oat Cookies

Day 3

Breakfast: Whole Grain French Toast
Lunch: Butternut Squash and Quinoa Stew
Dinner: Quinoa Stuffed Bell Peppers

Snacks: Whole Wheat Pretzel Bites
Dessert: Apple Cinnamon Oatmeal Bars

Breakfast: Protein-Packed Quinoa Breakfast Bowl
Lunch: Mediterranean Couscous Salad
Dinner: Lemon Herb Pasta with Shrimp

Breakfast: Cinnamon Swirl Bagels
Lunch: Veggie-Packed Burrito Bowl
Dinner: Hearty Vegetarian Lasagna

Breakfast: Maple-Sweetened Granola
Lunch: Grilled Chicken Pasta Salad
Dinner: Sweet Potato and Black Bean Chili

Breakfast: Berry Bliss Smoothie Bowl
Lunch: Black Bean and Corn Quesadillas
Dinner: Moroccan Lentil Stew

Breakfast: Veggie-Packed Breakfast Burritos
Lunch: Asian-Inspired Noodle Bowl
Dinner: Teriyaki Chicken and Rice Bowl

Breakfast: Sweet Potato and Black Bean Breakfast Hash
Lunch: Hearty Lentil Soup with Whole Grain Bread

Breakfast: Pumpkin Spice Oatmeal
Lunch: Sweet Potato Black Bean Burgers
Dinner: Greek Orzo with Grilled Vegetables

Breakfast: Maple-Sweetened Granola
Lunch: Veggie-Packed Burrito Bowl
Dinner: Teriyaki Chicken and Rice Bowl

Breakfast: Berry Bliss Smoothie Bowl
Lunch: Grilled Chicken Pasta Salad
Dinner: Greek Orzo with Grilled Vegetables

Breakfast: Pumpkin Spice Oatmeal
Lunch: Black Bean and Corn Quesadillas
Dinner: Quinoa Stuffed Bell Peppers

Breakfast: Banana and Blueberry Pancakes
Lunch: Lentil and Sweet Potato Salad
Dinner: Loaded Veggie Pizza

Day 4
Snacks: Apple Cinnamon Muffins
Dessert: Mixed Berry Cobbler

Day 5
Snacks: Peanut Butter Banana Smoothie
Dessert: Chocolate-Dipped Strawberries

Day 6
Snacks: Roasted Chickpea Snack Mix
Dessert: Almond Joy Energy Balls

Day 7
Snacks: Fruit and Nut Granola Bars
Dessert: Baked Apples with Cinnamon

Day 8
Snacks: Baked Zucchini Fries with Marinara
Dessert: Pumpkin Spice Donuts

Day 9
Dinner: Butternut Squash Mac and Cheese
Snacks: Oven-Roasted Edamame
Dessert: Chewy Maple Oat Clusters

Day 10
Snacks: Dark Chocolate Covered Almonds
Dessert: Vegan Chocolate Brownies

Day 11
Snacks: Dark Chocolate Covered Almonds
Dessert: Banana Bread Pudding

Day 12
Snacks: Oven-Roasted Edamame
Dessert: Dark Chocolate Chip Oat Cookies

Day 13
Snacks: Baked Sweet Potato Fries
Dessert: Apple Cinnamon Oatmeal Bars

Day 14
Snacks: Energy-Boosting Trail Mix
Dessert: Mixed Berry Cobbler

Breakfast: Oats and Apple Porridge
Lunch: Chickpea Avocado Toast
Dinner: Hearty Vegetarian Lasagna

Breakfast: Whole Grain French Toast
Lunch: Mediterranean Couscous Salad
Dinner: Sweet Potato and Black Bean Chili

Breakfast: Protein-Packed Quinoa Breakfast Bowl
Lunch: Butternut Squash and Quinoa Stew
Dinner: Moroccan Lentil Stew

Breakfast: Cinnamon Swirl Bagels
Lunch: Asian-Inspired Noodle Bowl
Dinner: Vegan Chickpea Curry with Brown Rice

Breakfast: Veggie-Packed Breakfast Burritos
Lunch: Hearty Lentil Soup with Whole Grain Bread
Dinner: Lemon Herb Pasta with Shrimp

Breakfast: Sweet Potato and Black Bean Breakfast Hash
Lunch: Sweet Potato Black Bean Burgers

Breakfast: Banana and Blueberry Pancakes
Lunch: Chickpea Avocado Toast
Dinner: Greek Orzo with Grilled Vegetables

Breakfast: Oats and Apple Porridge
Lunch: Butternut Squash and Quinoa Stew
Dinner: Hearty Vegetarian Lasagna

Breakfast: Whole Grain French Toast
Lunch: Mediterranean Couscous Salad
Dinner: Sweet Potato and Black Bean Chili

Breakfast: Protein-Packed Quinoa Breakfast Bowl
Lunch: Veggie-Packed Burrito Bowl
Dinner: Moroccan Lentil Stew

Breakfast: Cinnamon Swirl Bagels
Lunch: Grilled Chicken Pasta Salad
Dinner: Teriyaki Chicken and Rice Bowl

Day 15
Snacks: Whole Wheat Pretzel Bites
Dessert: Chocolate-Dipped Strawberries

Day 16
Snacks: Apple Cinnamon Muffins
Dessert: Almond Joy Energy Balls

Day 17
Snacks: Peanut Butter Banana Smoothie
Dessert: Baked Apples with Cinnamon

Day 18
Snacks: Roasted Chickpea Snack Mix
Dessert: Pumpkin Spice Donuts

Day 19
Snacks: Fruit and Nut Granola Bars
Dessert: Chewy Maple Oat Clusters

Day 20
Dinner: Butternut Squash Mac and Cheese
Snacks: Baked Zucchini Fries with Marinara
Dessert: Vegan Chocolate Brownies

Day 21
Snacks: Oven-Roasted Edamame
Dessert: Banana Bread Pudding

Day 22
Snacks: Dark Chocolate Covered Almonds
Dessert: Dark Chocolate Chip Oat Cookies

Day 23
Snacks: Baked Sweet Potato Fries
Dessert: Apple Cinnamon Oatmeal Bars

Day 24
Snacks: Energy-Boosting Trail Mix
Dessert: Mixed Berry Cobbler

Day 25
Snacks: Whole Wheat Pretzel Bites
Dessert: Chocolate-Dipped Strawberries

Breakfast: Maple-Sweetened Granola
Lunch: Black Bean and Corn Quesadillas
Dinner: Quinoa Stuffed Bell Peppers

Breakfast: Berry Bliss Smoothie Bowl
Lunch: Asian-Inspired Noodle Bowl
Dinner: Loaded Veggie Pizza

Breakfast: Pumpkin Spice Oatmeal
Lunch: Hearty Lentil Soup with Whole Grain Bread
Dinner: Vegan Chickpea Curry with Brown Rice

Breakfast: Veggie-Packed Breakfast Burritos
Lunch: Sweet Potato Black Bean Burgers
Dinner: Lemon Herb Pasta with Shrimp

Breakfast: Sweet Potato and Black Bean Breakfast Hash
Lunch: Lentil and Sweet Potato Salad

Day 26
Snacks: Apple Cinnamon Muffins
Dessert: Almond Joy Energy Balls

Day 27
Snacks: Peanut Butter Banana Smoothie
Dessert: Baked Apples with Cinnamon

Day 28
Snacks: Roasted Chickpea Snack Mix
Dessert: Pumpkin Spice Donuts

Day 29
Snacks: Fruit and Nut Granola Bars
Dessert: Chewy Maple Oat Clusters

Day 30
Dinner: Butternut Squash Mac and Cheese
Snacks: Baked Zucchini Fries with Marinara
Dessert: Vegan Chocolate Brownies

Low Carb Meal Plan

Day 1

Breakfast: Sunrise Spinach and Egg Muffins
Lunch: Crunchy Chicken Salad Wraps
Dinner: Garlic Butter Steak Bites

Snacks: Avocado Deviled Eggs
Dessert: Raspberry Almond Squares

Day 2

Breakfast: Avocado Stuffed Omelet
Lunch: Greek Style Cauliflower Rice Bowl
Dinner: Balsamic Chicken with Brussels Sprouts

Snacks: Smoked Salmon Cucumber Bites
Dessert: Flourless Chocolate Cake

Day 3

Breakfast: Zesty Zucchini Frittata
Lunch: Zucchini Noodle Pasta with Pesto
Dinner: Crispy Skin Salmon with Zoodles

Snacks: Spicy Roasted Almonds
Dessert: Lemon Cheesecake Bites

Day 4

Breakfast: Keto-friendly Pancakes
Lunch: Rainbow Vegetable Skewers
Dinner: Stuffed Bell Peppers with Ground Turkey

Snacks: Mediterranean Olives and Feta Skewers
Dessert: Keto Peanut Butter Cookies

Day 5

Breakfast: Almond Flour Breakfast Biscuits
Lunch: Spicy Shrimp and Avocado Lettuce Wraps
Dinner: Shrimp Scampi Spaghetti Squash

Snacks: Veggie Dippers with Hummus
Dessert: Low Carb Strawberry Shortcake

Day 6

Breakfast: Smoky Salmon and Cream Cheese Wrap
Lunch: Mediterranean Tuna Salad
Dinner: Low-Carb Chicken Alfredo

Snacks: Greek Yogurt Ranch Dip with Veggies
Dessert: Dark Chocolate Avocado Mousse

Breakfast: Low Carb Breakfast Burrito
Lunch: Egg Roll in a Bowl
Dinner: Spicy Mexican Cauliflower Rice

Breakfast: Sausage, Egg, and Cheese Bake
Lunch: Grilled Chicken Cobb Salad
Dinner: Sheet Pan Lemon Pepper Chicken

Breakfast: Powerhouse Protein Smoothie
Lunch: Crispy Baked Tofu Stir Fry
Dinner: Eggplant Parmesan Rollatini

Breakfast: Cauliflower Hash Browns
Lunch: Cheesy Spinach Stuffed Chicken Breast
Dinner: Grilled Portobello Mushroom Burgers

Breakfast: Avocado Stuffed Omelet
Lunch: Greek Style Cauliflower Rice Bowl
Dinner: Garlic Butter Steak Bites

Breakfast: Smoky Salmon and Cream Cheese Wrap
Lunch: Rainbow Vegetable Skewers
Dinner: Stuffed Bell Peppers with Ground Turkey

Breakfast: Low Carb Breakfast Burrito
Lunch: Crunchy Chicken Salad Wraps
Dinner: Crispy Skin Salmon with Zoodles

Breakfast: Sunrise Spinach and Egg Muffins
Lunch: Zucchini Noodle Pasta with Pesto
Dinner: Balsamic Chicken with Brussels Sprouts

Breakfast: Almond Flour Breakfast Biscuits
Lunch: Spicy Shrimp and Avocado Lettuce Wraps
Dinner: Low-Carb Chicken Alfredo

Breakfast: Powerhouse Protein Smoothie
Lunch: Mediterranean Tuna Salad
Dinner: Spicy Mexican Cauliflower Rice

Breakfast: Zesty Zucchini Frittata
Lunch: Egg Roll in a Bowl
Dinner: Eggplant Parmesan Rollatini

Day 7
Snacks: Keto Coconut Macaroons
Dessert: Cinnamon Almond Protein Bars

Day 8
Snacks: Mini Bell Pepper Nachos
Dessert: Coconut Cream Pie

Day 9
Snacks: Zucchini Chips with Guacamole
Dessert: Blueberry Lemon Ricotta Pancakes

Day 10
Snacks: Buffalo Chicken Celery Sticks
Dessert: Chocolate Almond Butter Fudge

Day 11
Snacks: Avocado Deviled Eggs
Dessert: Flourless Chocolate Cake

Day 12
Snacks: Mediterranean Olives and Feta Skewers
Dessert: Keto Peanut Butter Cookies

Day 13
Snacks: Smoked Salmon Cucumber Bites
Dessert: Lemon Cheesecake Bites

Day 14
Snacks: Spicy Roasted Almonds
Dessert: Low Carb Strawberry Shortcake

Day 15
Snacks: Greek Yogurt Ranch Dip with Veggies
Dessert: Dark Chocolate Avocado Mousse

Day 16
Snacks: Veggie Dippers with Hummus
Dessert: Cinnamon Almond Protein Bars

Day 17
Snacks: Mini Bell Pepper Nachos
Dessert: Blueberry Lemon Ricotta Pancakes

Breakfast: Sausage, Egg, and Cheese Bake
Lunch: Crispy Baked Tofu Stir Fry
Dinner: Sheet Pan Lemon Pepper Chicken

Breakfast: Keto-friendly Pancakes
Lunch: Grilled Chicken Cobb Salad
Dinner: Shrimp Scampi Spaghetti Squash

Breakfast: Sunrise Spinach and Egg Muffins
Lunch: Greek Style Cauliflower Rice Bowl
Dinner: Stuffed Bell Peppers with Ground Turkey

Breakfast: Avocado Stuffed Omelet
Lunch: Zucchini Noodle Pasta with Pesto
Dinner: Crispy Skin Salmon with Zoodles

Breakfast: Smoky Salmon and Cream Cheese Wrap
Lunch: Spicy Shrimp and Avocado Lettuce Wraps
Dinner: Low-Carb Chicken Alfredo

Breakfast: Powerhouse Protein Smoothie
Lunch: Mediterranean Tuna Salad
Dinner: Spicy Mexican Cauliflower Rice

Breakfast: Low Carb Breakfast Burrito
Lunch: Grilled Chicken Cobb Salad
Dinner: Eggplant Parmesan Rollatini

Breakfast: Sunrise Spinach and Egg Muffins
Lunch: Rainbow Vegetable Skewers
Dinner: Garlic Butter Steak Bites

Breakfast: Almond Flour Breakfast Biscuits
Lunch: Crunchy Chicken Salad Wraps
Dinner: Balsamic Chicken with Brussels Sprouts

Breakfast: Zesty Zucchini Frittata
Lunch: Cheesy Spinach Stuffed Chicken Breast
Dinner: Grilled Portobello Mushroom Burgers

Breakfast: Keto-friendly Pancakes
Lunch: Zucchini Noodle Pasta with Pesto
Dinner: Shrimp Scampi Spaghetti Squash

Day 18
Snacks: Buffalo Chicken Celery Sticks
Dessert: Chocolate Almond Butter Fudge

Day 19
Snacks: Keto Coconut Macaroons
Dessert: Coconut Cream Pie

Day 20
Snacks: Zucchini Chips with Guacamole
Dessert: Raspberry Almond Squares

Day 21
Snacks: Avocado Deviled Eggs
Dessert: Flourless Chocolate Cake

Day 22
Snacks: Mediterranean Olives and Feta Skewers
Dessert: Keto Peanut Butter Cookies

Day 23
Snacks: Greek Yogurt Ranch Dip with Veggies
Dessert: Lemon Cheesecake Bites

Day 24
Snacks: Veggie Dippers with Hummus
Dessert: Low Carb Strawberry Shortcake

Day 25
Snacks: Spicy Roasted Almonds
Dessert: Dark Chocolate Avocado Mousse

Day 26
Snacks: Smoked Salmon Cucumber Bites
Dessert: Cinnamon Almond Protein Bars

Day 27
Snacks: Mini Bell Pepper Nachos
Dessert: Blueberry Lemon Ricotta Pancakes

Day 28
Snacks: Buffalo Chicken Celery Sticks
Dessert: Chocolate Almond Butter Fudge

Breakfast: Avocado Stuffed Omelet
Lunch: Greek Style Cauliflower Rice Bowl
Dinner: Stuffed Bell Peppers with Ground Turkey

Breakfast: Sausage, Egg, and Cheese Bake
Lunch: Crunchy Chicken Salad Wraps
Dinner: Crispy Skin Salmon with Zoodles

Day 29

Snacks: Zucchini Chips with Guacamole
Dessert: Raspberry Almond Squares

Day 30

Snacks: Avocado Deviled Eggs
Dessert: Flourless Chocolate Cake

Useful Apps for Calorie Calculation

Calculating your calorie intake can be vital when it comes to following a diet plan. The process can be simplified by using certain mobile apps that not only track calories but also monitor macronutrients, provide exercise routines, offer recipe suggestions, and a lot more. Here are some useful apps for calorie calculation:

1. **MyFitnessPal**: It's a widely-used app that has an enormous database of more than 6 million foods. You can log the food you eat by scanning the barcode on packaged foods or by manually finding them in the database. MyFitnessPal also tracks your water intake, exercise, and more.
2. **Lose It!**: This app lets you set a goal weight and suggests a daily calorie budget to help you achieve it. You can track your food intake and exercise, view detailed reports about your nutrition, and celebrate your successes along the way.
3. **FatSecret**: FatSecret offers a monthly summary view that provides the total calories consumed each day, total fats, and more. It features a vibrant community where users can share their successes, ideas, and recipes.
4. **Cronometer**: If you're into tracking micronutrients—like vitamins and minerals—Cronometer might be the best choice for you. It tracks over 60 micronutrients, ensuring you get the right balance of vitamins and minerals.
5. **Yazio**: This is a multi-platform calorie counter that provides a wide range of nutritional information. The Pro version also provides a more comprehensive breakdown of daily nutrition and the ability to switch between multiple high and low-carb days.
6. **Lifesum**: Lifesum offers a personalized roadmap to better health, meaning you get a diet plan that is suited for you. Besides counting calories, it allows you to track macros, sugar, fiber, and cholesterol, making it easier for you to make healthy choices.
7. **Noom**: This app focuses on making lifelong healthy habits, not just losing weight. You track your food and exercise in Noom, but the app focuses on behavioral changes more than just the numbers.

Shopping List

Vegetables/Fruits

- Spinach
- Avocado
- Zucchini
- Lemon
- Cauliflower
- Lettuce
- Bell peppers (all colors)
- Brussels sprouts
- Garlic
- Olives
- Cucumber
- Mushrooms

- Sweet potato
- Black beans
- Blueberries
- Apples
- Bananas
- Pumpkin
- Carrots
- Tomatoes
- Onion
- Butternut squash
- Celery
- Berries (for smoothies and salads)

Grains

- Almond flour
- Whole grain bread
- Oats
- Quinoa
- Whole grain pasta

- Couscous
- Brown rice
- Orzo
- Whole wheat pretzels
- Granola

Proteins

- Eggs
- Salmon
- Chicken (breast, thighs)
- Ground turkey
- Shrimp
- Tofu
- Sausage
- Steak

Dairy

- Cheese (cheddar, mozzarella, cream cheese, feta)
- Greek yogurt
- Butter
- Ricotta
- Milk (regular and almond)

Canned Goods

- Tuna
- Chickpeas
- Corn
- Lentils
- Marinara sauce

Nuts/Seeds

- Almonds
- Trail mix (variety)
- Peanut butter
- Macaroons
- Edamame

Spices/Oils

- Olive oil
- Balsamic vinegar
- Spices (salt, black pepper, cayenne pepper, chili powder, cinnamon, nutmeg, cumin, oregano, basil, etc.)
- Honey
- Maple syrup
- Dark chocolate

Others

- Whole grain bagels
- Protein powder
- Coconut cream
- Protein bars

Conclusion

As we come to the end of this comprehensive guide to carb cycling, it's crucial to remember that our journey toward health and fitness is a marathon, not a sprint. Adopting a new dietary approach is not about rapid, dramatic changes. Instead, it's about sustainable adaptations that can be maintained in the long run, fueling our bodies optimally while enhancing our quality of life.

Through this book, we have ventured into the intriguing world of carb cycling, demystifying its complexities and highlighting its potential benefits. We have examined how strategically cycling our carbohydrate intake can amplify our athletic performance, promote fat loss, and even enhance cognitive function. The comprehensive meal plans, coupled with diverse, mouth-watering recipes, have shown us that a health-focused diet does not mean sacrificing the pleasure of eating.

Carb Cycling is not a magic bullet or a one-size-fits-all solution. It is a flexible nutritional tool that can be adjusted to individual goals, lifestyles, and preferences. This is where the essence of carb cycling truly shines – its adaptability. By understanding your body's needs and learning to listen to its signals, you can personalize your carb cycling regimen to fit you perfectly.

Remember, the key to success with carb cycling, as with any dietary approach, lies in consistency and patience. Allow yourself the grace to make mistakes and learn from them. Celebrate your small victories and learnings along the way. And above all, keep in mind that our dietary choices are just one piece of the larger health puzzle, with other aspects like regular physical activity, adequate sleep, stress management, and a positive mindset being equally important.

As you close this book and embark on your carb-cycling journey, keep the words of ancient philosopher Hippocrates in mind: "Let food be thy medicine and medicine be thy food." Here's to making the most of your carb cycling experience, paving the way toward peak performance, optimal health, and a life brimming with vitality.

Thank you for choosing *Carb Cycling* as your guide on this journey. May the insights, strategies, and recipes shared within these pages illuminate your path, and may your carb-cycling adventure be rewarding, enlightening, and delicious. Happy carb cycling!

Printed in Great Britain
by Amazon

42642896R00066